THE CHURCH AND SEX

IS VOLUME

103

OF THE

Twentieth Century Encyclopedia of Catholicism

UNDER SECTION

IX

*THE CHURCH AND THE MODERN WORLD*

IT IS ALSO THE

37TH

VOLUME IN ORDER OF PUBLICATION

*Edited by* **HENRI DANIEL-ROPS** *of the Académie Française*

# THE CHURCH AND SEX

## By R. F. TREVETT

HAWTHORN BOOKS · PUBLISHERS · New York

*First Edition,* March, 1960
*Second Printing,* January, 1961
*Third Printing,* May, 1963
*Fourth Printing,* March, 1965

NIHIL OBSTAT

Adrianus Van Vliet, S.T.D.

*Censor Deputatus*

IMPRIMATUR

E. Morrogh Bernard

*Vicarius Generalis*

Westmonasterii, die XXXI OCTOBRIS MCMLIX

The Nihil obstat and Imprimatur are a declaration that a book or pamphlet is considered to be free from doctrinal or moral error. It is not implied that those who have granted the Nihil obstat and Imprimatur agree with the contents, opinions or statements expressed.

H-9460

# CONTENTS

# INTRODUCTION

There is no getting away from sex. We are all men or women and our whole life is profoundly affected by our sexuality. We cannot brush it to one side nor pretend that only scientists, doctors and theologians need to think about it. Although these experts have much to say on the subject, most of their observations seem to have little to do with life in general or sex life in particular. We are inclined to feel that sex is a personal affair and that we shall not go far wrong if we follow our natural instincts. We do not require other people's advice in so intimate a matter.

The title of this book may therefore puzzle us. What has Christianity to do with sex? We know that marriage is a sacrament but sacraments are spiritual things. The physical basis of marriage is included in the sacrament of matrimony. It cannot be otherwise, but to talk of a specifically Christian approach to sex itself seems as pointless as to talk of a Christian approach to farming or cooking. We accept the Church's teaching on chastity, divorce and contraception, yet we sometimes feel that it indicates a negative attitude to a great physical urge. We wonder whether moral theologians who, after all, are celibates can really understand or appreciate the difficulties we meet in our sex life.

Even if we are unaware of it, our own attitude to sex is to some extent conditioned by the "sexual climate" of our times. We perhaps avoid sins against the sixth commandment, but we may think that the Church's rigid code takes little or no account of the facts of life. We hear an occasional sermon on marriage at a wedding or during a mission. At the former what is said seems either sentimental, "pious" or academic; at the latter, we are harangued about the law and the dire consequences of disobeying it. We remember solemn warnings during our school life and how pointless they seemed when we left the classroom for the factory or the office. There our companions managed to combine goodness in their general dealings with a free and easy sex code. We know of young men and women who have sexual experience before marriage and yet become excellent wives, husbands, mothers and fathers. Married couples who practise contraception seem as happy and healthy as those who do not. Men and women who have divorced and remarried have found happiness in a second union. What then is all this fuss about sex in the catechism and the pulpit? We have an occasional sneaking wish that the laws of the Church might be modified. Not that we would have any truck with adultery or divorce as such, but surely there is room for more tolerance towards those struggling with a very powerful instinct that is apparently always warring against principles which seem unable of themselves to stem the upsurge of the passions.

The writer of this book is a layman, a husband and a father. He will not minimize the difficulties the above objections reveal. These objections exist even if they are not always stated so frankly and openly. This book like the others in the series deals with the Catholic Faith in relation to the facts of the present-day situation, especially in Great Britain and the United States. There is no point in plunging our heads into the sand. We must face the world in which our Christian attitude to sex has to make its mark. We have, as baptized and confirmed members of Christ, to preach the Gospel through and in our sex lives as well as in and through the other departments of our complicated existence.

God has created us men and women. Our Lord has redeemed our whole nature. Sex is not left to the world, the flesh and the devil. When we ask, "What is the Christian attitude to sex?" we mean, what is God's purpose in making us sexual creatures? Why is our sex life bedevilled with problems? Are those problems genuine or the result of taboos? What has Christ done that our sexuality is now included in our sacramental life? If we can find positive and practical answers to these questions, we may hope also to discover something very different from the negation and prudery, the obscurantism and intolerance which many sincerely believe—and we Catholics must take our share of the blame for this sorry state of affairs—make up the Church's teaching on sex. If we can find a solid doctrine with real bearing on life as it has to be lived, we may hope to be apostles not in spite of but through our sexuality.

We are certain God has not made us male and female for solely biological purposes. The difficulties of our sex life must have some meaning, some value, some relevance to the life of grace. We have had enough of Sunday piety and the Christian-shut-up-in-the-castle mentality. We cannot go on for ever trying to reconcile papal encyclicals on marriage with the Hollywood code by which most of our friends more or less live. The latter appear to think sex has two functions which can be kept separate. It is a mechanism for having children, and it is a source of intense pleasure. If the two can be combined, well and good, if not, why worry? Marriage and parenthood are one thing and sex life another and much bigger one. If you want to keep them together, good luck to you! If not, what is there to stop you? Nature and human ingenuity make it possible for joy to be unconfined in all senses of the word. By what right do priests attempt to keep together what nature and man can obviously put asunder? Marriage is a useful institution, we grant you that, but it is like schools, factories, the National Health Service, and life is more than education, work and hospitals. In sex there is more than marriage, childbirth and the rearing of children. Sex belongs also to the world of "fun", entertainment, amusement, "thrills", pleasure. The myths of a primitive Semitic tribe are out of date in the twentieth century.

Mere pious exhortation, mere negative warnings are useless against this sort of barrage. We must look for weapons in a better armoury. Peter Maurin never tired of calling on Catholics, clerical and lay, to bring out what he would now surely call, were he alive, the "nuclear" forces of the Church's doctrine. Only truth can shatter falsehood, only the dynamic force of revelation can bring all that is genuine and good in the modern desire for a human and humane approach to love and sex into the great creative and redemptive synthesis which our Lord has achieved for our race. If this book can give a few pointers to this living spring of doctrine, it will have served its purpose.

*Taunton*
*June 29th*, 1959

# PART I

# THE FACTS OF FAITH

CHAPTER I

# SEX BEFORE THE FALL

If there was no Fall, Christianity is nonsense. This is a hard saying and must be justified. We think perhaps that if man goes on making scientific experiments, he will find out all the secrets of the universe. The greatest scientists are none too sure of this. They see that the philosopher's queries about the human mind and its power to know have to be met and that they cannot be met by experiment alone. Science cannot prove its own first principles. It can only show that they give results. The fact that a theory of any kind works does not mean that everything will be eventually explained. We may imagine that scientists survey the whole field of reality, but perhaps there are equally if not more important facts beyond the scope of their research. If we say this is impossible, we are arguing unscientifically; we are proclaiming a dogma.

This is not to attack science but to defend it against the kind of false thinking which might one day prove its ruin. It is not unreasonable to suppose that there are mysteries beyond its reach, and not only mysteries in the religious or philosophical sense. The theologian Scheeben points out that even the simplest objects of natural knowledge remain mysterious for us in some respects.[1] Science itself springs from the fact that nature is full of mysteries about

[1] *The Mysteries of Christianity*, English translation, St Louis, Mo., and London, Herder, 1947, p. 8.

which we can indeed discover something but which will continually offer realities still unknown, thus urging the scientist to further experiment and theory. Yet an ultimate mystery always remains, for man cannot stand completely outside himself and observe and describe with absolute objectivity his own knowledge in its relations to reality.

Science has discovered much about human nature, its evolution, its physical and mental functioning, and will continue to discover still more. This knowledge is important and valuable, but we have no right to assume that scientific research is the only source of information about man. To many of our contemporaries, the scientific hypothesis of organic evolution has said the last word on human nature—and consequently about human sexuality. Religion may have been necessary as a pre-scientific mythology, it can no longer claim to impart knowledge. The Fall of man is a myth. Christianity today may have some relevance in the fields of human conduct, politics, economics and social obligations, it may help to make life easier and more pleasant; it can tell us nothing about the root facts of human existence.

Such a doctrine has no scientific basis, it is a dogmatic assumption. As such, Christians must reckon and deal with it. They will not deny the validity and value of scientific discovery, but they will have a total view of reality based on the facts not only of science but also on those of Christ's life, teaching and purposes. The fact of the Fall will be known by revelation. It will not contradict whatever is true in the evolutionary theories. It will merely deny that these theories tell the whole story. In this book we are not primarily concerned with justifying the Christian position in regard to knowledge. That has been done elsewhere in the series. We merely insist that this position is as rational as that of the scientific dogmatist.

To return then to our starting-point. The Fall is essential

for the understanding of what Christianity is about. Adam
and Christ are the two universal men. We are born in
Adam and reborn in Christ. Adam's Fall and Christ's Redemption are ultimate mysteries, realities known to us
solely through God's revelation and then only "in part".
We cannot discover them by natural means nor find
rational concepts adequate to represent them.[2]

The Fall and the Redemption are facts beyond the scope
of all research. This should not disturb us. We have already
seen that there are "natural" mysteries. In the matter of
sex, for instance, scientific investigation has revealed a
host of facts concerning genes, chromosomes, the phenomena that have given rise to the hypothesis of the
Oedipus complex, sociological pressures on marriage
customs and sexual morals, etc. Yet sex as a natural phenomenon is likely to retain certain mysterious aspects
however much our knowledge may increase—its relation
to love for example. The Fall is a mystery beyond human
discovery, yet its effects upon our daily life, upon our
natural existence and knowledge are primordial. It makes
some of the natural mysteries less obscure, since the least
grain of truth about man's relations with God and with
other men in God is of infinitely greater value, both in
itself and to us, than the whole body of natural knowledge,
for it leads us to the realm of the abiding, the eternal, the
ultimate reality.

The Fall doctrine describes man's first estate and the
original sin which destroyed it. It would be a gross error
to imagine this sin to have been sexual. Nevertheless man's
total subsequent evolution—and this includes his sex life—
was altered by the fact of the Fall. It is equally true that
Christ's Redemption has repercussions in the field of sex.
In these first three chapters we attempt to descry some of
the implications of these two cosmic supernatural events

[2] See Scheeben, *op. cit.*, p. 13.

upon the sexuality of mankind. We contemplate the mysteries of creation in grace, of original sin and redemption as they affect our sex life. In the chapters that follow we shall examine our situation here and now in the light of these mysteries and suggest answers to the questions—what has Christianity to say about sex? what can Christians do about their sex life in the modern world?

If we are to have some idea of the rôle of sexuality in human life before the Fall, we must consider the general situation of Adam in the state of innocence. God had raised man from his natural status as a rational animal to that of divine sonship, to a share in the life of the Holy Trinity itself. Adam was holy, or rather, he had in him the seed of holiness which was to flower into a final, complete and indestructible union with God. The mystery of sin cannot be contemplated unless we realize first that this supernatural holiness was absolutely above and beyond the natural situation of Adam; it was God's free gift of an altogether superhuman perfection. With it came another —integrity—which kept the various forces in human nature in harmony with one another. It guaranteed man against the physical dissolution inseparable from his material, bodily existence. He was protected, that is, both from the centrifugal forces of passion rooted in his physical being and clamouring for independence, and also against the natural processes of disease and degeneration which eventually destroy the body.

Adam and Eve's original integrity and holiness made their sexuality holy and in line with their sonship in God. The Holy Spirit united them directly to himself in the process of generation. Every child born of their union was to inherit their supernatural state. Through their mysterious oneness with God their nature was to be the means by which the future race was to be born in sonship with

God. Such a vocation required the grace of integrity. Otherwise the natural tendency of the passions to seek their own aims regardless of the general good of the human person would have thwarted God's purposes for man at the very root of his nature.

The Genesis narrative and our Lord's teaching on marriage make it clear that this supernatural vocation for which man's sexuality was destined was shared between both partners. Their physical union in the sex acts was subordinated to Adam's status as head of the race. Matter in human nature was to be the instrument of both the natural and the supernatural purposes of the holy, creative and sanctifying Spirit. The unity and harmony in Adam's soul was to be extended to the unity of man and woman in marriage. They were to be one flesh. In their state of supernatural holiness, this meant far more than just a cooperation of body and soul. Their union was involved in the union of man to God in sonship. The comparison sometimes made between the unity of the three persons of the Trinity and that of father, mother and child in the human family is of value if rightly understood. Adam and Eve were partakers of the divine nature. In the world of creatures their union with one another and with their children was to be a figure of the union of the divine persons.

The sense of the Genesis narrative can only be fully grasped if read in the light of the New Testament. St Paul's great chapter in his epistle to the Ephesians reveals the inner meaning of the Old Testament declaration: "They shall be two in one flesh." St Paul writes: "Man is the head to which the body of the woman is united, just as Christ is the head of the Church, he, the Saviour on whom the safety of his body depends."[3] We shall return to this doctrine later. For the moment, we note that it shows that

[3] Ephes. 5. 23.

marriage in Eden implied far more than physical cooperation in a biological act, however much the latter was lifted
above nature to become part of the divine vocation of
Adam. The union of Christ and the Church, his body, is
based on the physical fact of his divine humanity, but it
is a union of souls, of persons, of love and mutual sacrifice.
As Christ has given himself to man, so man is to give himself to Christ and through Christ to the Father in and
through the Spirit. So too, Adam's union with Eve was
one of pure, unselfish love, a love so holy and spiritual
that all the physical phenomena of sexuality were completely included in and subordinated to it.

Adam and Eve were naked and unashamed. They had
nothing to be ashamed of. Shame is one of the fruits of
sin. In each of them body and soul were in perfect union
and their marriage act was one of utter love. This did
not mean that the sex acts were any less physical. St
Thomas says that the pleasure involved was far more
intense than that which fallen man can experience, precisely because it was not self-centred and self-seeking.
When pleasure is sought out of inordinate desire, it brings
with it an element of discontent and frustration. The
pleasure which Adam and Eve knew in their sexual love
had no such drawbacks.

It was from this love that children were to be born. As
the creation of the universe and all that is in it is an
act of pure, disinterested love on God's part, so the procreation of children was to be in and through the holiness,
justice and love which Adam had received from him. The
sons of men were to be born sons of God through the love
of man for woman, and by means of the physical acts
whereby that love was to inscribe itself on the material
universe. The world of matter travails and groans for the
revelation of the sons of God. It is in the love of man for
God, of man and woman for each other in and through

God, that the physical universe itself is to be lifted up to supernatural union with its Creator. Man is king and priest of the world of things.

Christians can therefore never think of sex as a purely animal phenomenon. In the beginning, as St Augustine puts it, "the raising of Adam to fellowship with the Holy Spirit . . . changed him from an 'animal man' to a 'spiritual man' ".[4] When we hear sex described as a "natural" thing, when we find people trying to justify an instinctual sex life untrammelled by any so-called taboos, we have to remember that their arguments are only valid if man is and always has been simply and solely a natural creature, an "animal man". The more common view nowadays, however, is that while he is no more than just this, yet the evolution of mind has placed him in an awkward predicament. The other animals, it is held, are controlled by instinct in their sexual activity. Man has acquired intelligence of a special kind or at a higher level. He can no longer lead a purely instinctual life. He has to control matter—and this includes his own body and its biological urges—by acts of will depending on the knowledge he acquires by his intellect. This view is part indeed of the whole truth, but as it stands it is an over-simplification.

The Christian must avoid a similar over-simplification by refusing to argue that man's troubles with his warring passions are a strict proof of his original innocence. We cannot reason here from effect to cause. Nothing is gained by trying to do so. The mystery of Adam's holiness and integrity cannot be known by an analysis of man's present status and struggle, but only by revelation. Man might have remained purely animal in St Augustine's sense and yet have evolved into a rational status without possessing any supernatural gifts. God is not bound to create us in sanctity, integrity, immortality. That he has done so can

[4] Scheeben, *op. cit.*, p. 215.

never be revealed by biological, historical, psychological research. It is dishonest to found an apologetic on a foundation which fails to include this fact. Natural human knowledge is one thing, knowledge by revelation another.

It is true, however, that once we grasp what the Fall involves, we shall see that it did much more than reduce or return man to a purely natural existence. His nature has been injured by sin in ways that would otherwise have been impossible. There is a perversion of the will which is inconceivable in a creature who has merely rebelled against the order of nature.[5] To order our lives on the assumption that we are or have become again purely natural men is to base our existence on an illusion. As Chesterton wrote, the glad good news of the Gospel is the news of original sin. This is profoundly true, for the doctrine of the Redemption is meaningless apart from the original innocence which it restores.

In a word, man did not lose his first vocation, though he did lose the holiness and integrity which made it possible and easy for him to fulfil it. Hence his sexuality is marked with the sign of supernatural love and is irrevocably called to cooperate in the creative work of the Holy Spirit. This is made clear in the mystery of Christ's virginal conception in the womb of the Blessed Virgin. In this direct intervention of the Spirit in the biological process of human conception, the real and ultimate sense of human sexuality is revealed. Man inherits his separation from God through his descent from Adam. Only a direct intervention of the Holy Spirit restores the original sanctity of sex. Nor was this done only when our Lord was conceived. His mother also was at her conception preserved from the results of Adam's Fall so far as sanctity and justice were concerned. The conception of our Lady and that of her son reveal the original glory of human sexuality. It was and is and always

[5] See Scheeben, *op. cit.*, p. 265.

will be the means whereby the love of the Spirit for mankind is made fruitful in the birth of new persons through the love of husband and wife. Sex is an instrument for the sanctification of the unborn generations. Its original, ultimate and abiding purpose is to give these birth in the fellowship of the Trinity.

# CHAPTER II

# SEX AFTER THE FALL

The devil is now a figure of fun. To say we believe he is a person is to invite a look of pity or a burst of laughter. Yet perhaps with memories of Belsen and Auschwitz still vivid, people may be more willing than they were to recognize that deeds so evil seem beyond the nature of man. If such crimes are to be explained solely in terms of human depravity, there is little hope for the future. If, on the other hand, man encounters demonic forces from without, if his warfare is not against flesh and blood, but against those spirits of wickedness in the high places with whom Christ has fought the final and victorious battle then, even though we tremble, we may believe and hope.

There is a striking parallel between the temptations of Adam and those of our Lord. The similarity lies both in the persons involved, Adam, Eve, Christ, Satan, and in the character of the temptations themselves. By examining the Gospel story we may grasp something of the mystery of the original Fall and its consequences in the realm of sex. We have at the same time to remember that our Lord could not suffer temptation from disordered or disorderly passions, as we can and do. In him as perfect man the flesh was wholly subservient to the spirit. Nor could he know pride and all the rebellious motions of the human heart. for he was the eternal Son of God.

Adam and Eve were asked three questions: Why have
you been forbidden to eat of the fruit of the tree of knowledge of good and evil? Why would this be wrong? Do
you not know that if you eat it you will be as gods knowing
good and evil? The devil attacks Christ in a similar way.
Will you not satisfy your hunger by changing these stones
into bread? Why not prove you are the Messiah by throwing
yourself from this pinnacle? Do you want to conquer the
world? If so, you need only fall down and worship me.

For Adam the business of the tree and its forbidden fruit
was no mere totem mystery, it concerned man's relations
with the rest of creation. Although a creature, Adam was
to be in a sense the vicar of Christ the Word through
whom all things are made. Our Lord did not answer Satan
as Son of God but as Son of Man under the Law. Adam
and Eve made no answer at all, they listened and waited
for more. Our Lord rebuked Satan—it is not for man to
attempt the absurd, to pretend he can arraign God before
him and give him commands. The primary absurdity of
evil, its inner core of nothingness could not be more clearly
revealed than in Satan's third temptation of Christ, for if
Christ worships the devil, his whole work will be ruined
at the source. Equally absurd were the devil's words to
Adam and Eve—you shall be as gods knowing good and
evil, as though by listening to Satan they would become
the masters of the universe and the equals of God who
knows both good and evil and is no less God for the evil
which he knows! Our Lord replied with a cry of anger:
"Away with you! Man must worship and serve God
only." But Adam and Eve took the fruit and ate. Their
eyes were opened and they were ashamed because they
were naked.

How did the Fall affect our sexuality? No differently
surely than it does the rest of our nature and life. The
temptations of Christ reveal the aim of the devil in our

affairs. They are simply stated. He is out to make us consider the universe as one vast object to be subdued to our
power; to make us forestall the divine will; to make us
optimists in the bad sense of the word. We will take risks
and God will clear up the mess for us. Finally, he is out
to persuade us that the only way to success is through the
illusory independence and self-centred power which he
himself desires in order to dominate God's creation.

Now that we are fallen, we experience our physical,
sexual urges as forces seeking their own ends, apart from
the general good of the whole personality. We tend to
consider the bodies of others as objects for our pleasure
or for our economic and social purposes. We are tempted
to see our sexuality as a source of power over others. If
we are men, we find we are needed to give woman's genital
instincts their legitimate outlet. If we are women, we know
the power we can wield over the strong passions of men.
We are led to argue that sex being what it is, an instinctual
drive, there is nothing we can do but to give it its head.
God or nature presumably knew what they were doing
when they evolved it for the reproduction of living physical
organisms. Let them solve the problems it raises! Meanwhile, we will enjoy it as much as we can. We marry,
divorce, commit adultery, masturbate, practise contraception, lead a sex life which assures us the maximum of
pleasure and the least bother and suffering. Finally, the
urge to success through power makes us use our sexuality
as a means of personal domination over others. In its extreme manifestation, this leads to sadism in the sexual act.
But, though in less virulent forms, it is present in all those
cases where men and women build their sex lives on the
quest for power, for so-called self-realization rather than
on unselfish love, devotion and sacrifice. In a word, the
loss of our integrity has led to a tearing apart of our own
personalities and of the web of relationships we were

destined to have with others in our original state of holiness and justice.

The Fall returns us to the world of the struggle for existence, the world of the evolving psyche; it also leaves us with a wound in our nature. Far more than instinct is needed if we are to avoid a descent into utter personal and social chaos. So arises the austere yet inevitable figure of the Law. Human societies legislate and their enactments are far more burdensome than the simple, unique command of God in Eden. Yet, in their hard and bitter way, they are a bulwark against the demonic forces which sweep across the soul of man and drive him to lust, hatred and murder. In the complex pattern of the Mosaic Code with its social, hygienic, economic, religious and personal laws, God revealed himself to Israel and prepared his people for the coming of Christ. At the same time, it made it possible for the faithful Hebrew in his relations with others to practise the love of God and his neighbour. For the Law looks back to the Fall, rescues the present from destruction and foresees the future Redemption. It is, as St Paul teaches, an interim measure, a schoolmaster, a pedagogue leading men to Christ.

The Law forbids the sexual sins. It attempts to do for man what instinct does for the brute beasts, to supply a norm by which we can lead our sex lives without grave harm to others and to ourselves. It gives legal form to one of the great projects of the human spirit—the bringing of the sex instinct in man into the service of love. The heart of the Law is love, and the deepest purpose of our sexuality must be to express the love we have for our creator and for his creatures. It is on this high project that the family as such is always engaged. The family is constantly solicited on the one hand by the call to love, and on the other by the urge to selfishness. It is in the family that the great human options present themselves continually in an acute and

unavoidable form. As E. Wellisch has shown in his book
*Isaac and Oedipus*, the story of Abraham and his consent
to the sacrifice of Isaac is the first recorded call to fallen
man to love creatures in God. In every family the "turning
of the hearts of the fathers to the children and of the
hearts of the children to the fathers" demands a complete
sacrifice of self in a love for God without which our love
for creatures is imperfect and full of danger for both those
who love and those who are loved. Small wonder, then,
that the Mosaic Law has so much to say about the regulation of family relationships and the duties and rights of
the members of that primal human institution which the
family is.

But, we may ask, how can so personal and intimate a
business as sexual union be regulated by a code imposed
from without? Does not the power of the Law lie in its
sanctions? We avoid sexual misconduct because we are
afraid of the social consequences of disobedience. It is
fear, not love, which presides over our sexual relations.
We think of the Law as opposed to liberty. The fear of
punishment, physical or moral, which law implies, seems
opposed to the free exercise of the will. We do what we
are told because we are afraid. But this is not the whole
story. In so far as the Law binds us, we lose something of
our personal freedom, yet, at the same time, the Law
frees us to some extent from the chaotic domination of
the passions. It helps us to acquire a limited natural integrity, an ordered, rational life. It saves us from slavery
to emotions, lusts, passions, which if they remained unchecked, would ultimately deprive the race of personality,
of any existence which could be properly called human.

In man's first state of holiness and integrity, sexuality
was the instrument of love. Now it tends to take the place
of love, to separate us from others instead of uniting us
to them. In the Trinity, the three persons by their mutual

self-giving are one and yet distinct in personality. So, though at an infinitely lower and creaturely level, man and woman were to deepen one another's personality by their mutual, self-denying love, expressed in a thousand ways, but in its fullness and most fruitful form through the genital act issuing in the new person of the child. This original vocation is fully restored and made even nobler by the Incarnation and the Redemption.

But to this high theme we are not yet ready to turn. We still have the Law to account for. In spite of its obvious value, its weaknesses cannot fail to affect our whole attitude to sex. Law is concerned with social purposes. It strives to keep the community from disintegrating; it cannot be primarily occupied with the growth of personalities, though it may provide favourable circumstances for such development. It cannot tell us how we are to love one another. It can only instruct us as to what *not* to do when we are in love. Its chief concern will be to prevent us from harming the race, from prejudicing the good of society at large. We shall not be surprised if it looks on sex as almost entirely biological and sociological. We feel that there is a contradiction here between what we know human love to be and the racial ends which the Law insists that it should serve.

This contradiction is a direct outcome of the Fall. In Eden there was no cleavage between love and fruitfulness. Adam and Eve were united to the Holy Spirit who is the source both of grace and of the generation of creatures.[1] The Holy Spirit is love. The union of our first parents was filled with the presence and power of Eternal Love. The Fall changed all this. Fallen man cannot love with all his soul. He has returned to the world of struggle which he was originally destined to rule in and through love. Love of self is now divorced from love of others. Man is no

[1] See Scheeben, *op. cit.*, p. 599.

longer the living sign of the ineffable love of the three
persons of the Trinity, he is part and parcel of the world
of creatures who groan for the "revelation of the sons of
God". He is like the prodigal son, forced to be content
with the husks of creaturely comforts that restore something approaching self-esteem. Nor would it be wrong to
compare the Law with these "husks" in so far as it is a
substitute for love.

This does not mean that until the Incarnation men and
women could not be in love and give birth to children in
and through their love. Man's vocation is not cancelled
by the Fall. The means by which it was to be fulfilled were
rejected by a mysterious yet responsible and free act of
Adam's will. His nature was wounded and only desperate
remedies such as the Law could relieve in some measure
his tragic situation. Yet individuals could and did rise
above the letter of the Law and recapture something of the
love which is at its heart. The idea of God as wedding
Israel made possible the love poem of the Song of Songs,
in which "love ... does not take the person away from his
life-work but on the contrary makes love incarnate there".[2]

In the same chapter Guitton comments on Plato's "Banquet," perhaps the greatest attempt made without revelation
to fathom the mystery of human love. For Plato, love is
man's way of escape from creaturehood. Through it he
rises above the world of sense and in an ecstasy of contemplation, sees and is one with the good, the true, the
beautiful, the source of all that is. For Plato this love
begins in the world of the body yet not in the relations of
man and woman but in homosexual passion. His insight
perceived that man is a scandal to woman and woman to
man, since their love appears to be a mere urge to perform
a biological, racial function. It is only by divorcing love

[2] Jean Guitton, *Essay on Human Love*, translated by Melville
Channing-Pearce, London, Rockliff, 1951.

from such purposes that, in the context of the "Banquet",
it can be purified.

So we inherit this division, this conflict in the mind,
between love and generation, between mutual self-giving
and the procreation of children. At all periods of history
we find men and women torn between the desire for one
another's bodies and the longing for true union in love.
How can these be reconciled? Law answers with its dictum
about the primary ends of marriage and with its regula-
tions and penalties. But the problem remains unsolved. We
have found only a *modus vivendi*, a reasonably convenient
arrangement which makes society possible. Without Law
our sexuality would fail to evolve, would stay fixed at a
sub-human level. We are grateful to the lawgivers but are
still at war with ourselves in that inner region where the
writ of Law cannot run. For, whether we know it or not,
our original vocation stands. We are destined to be the
prophets, priests and kings of nature through the love of
the Spirit which united our first parents. Law cannot for
ever hold us back. Our nature cries out for the Redeemer.
And in Christ we are restored to our former glory. In him
we become again holy, whole, one with ourselves, one with
each other, one with God. In him our bodily life, our
sexuality return to the realm of perfect love. Further, our
original vocation is made immeasurably nobler. It is raised
to a still more sublime status in Christ, for from henceforth,
*man and woman are to be the sign of his union with the
human race.* We live in the world of grace and of the sacrament of marriage in which love and generation are again
made one.

# CHAPTER III

# SEX AND THE
# REDEMPTION

"I being lifted up will draw all things to myself," said our Lord. The God-man has redeemed sex. Through him it enters into a real, sublime relation to the life of the Trinity, nobler than that of Eden.

Christian faith, Christian life, the structure, worship and teaching of the Christian Church spring from one primordial fact—Jesus Christ is true God and true man. In him, our humanity is deified, caught up into the inner life of the Trinity. By the fact of his Incarnation, he assumed human nature into union with the divine nature in himself. Once assumed therein it can never again be separated from it. By becoming man, God the Son has placed within a human soul all the power, majesty and purity of the Godhead. In him, as St Paul says, the fullness of the Godhead dwells bodily. His human nature is the instrument of his divine nature. Through it grace flows into our whole race. Through it each one of us is destined to union with the Father here in faith and, in the life to come, in everlasting glory.

Adam is the point at which the race began, the means whereby future generations were to be born into that supernatural manhood to which our "animal" nature had been raised by God's decree. Neither the state nor the grace were Adam's to give. But the humanity of God the Son, at one with his divinity, is the source of grace, the root and ground of redemption, the eternal pledge of our union with the Godhead. Its acts have a value that is infinite and wholly efficacious. By our oneness with Christ, we are filled with grace, we become other Christs. He is the Head of the race in a far deeper sense than Adam. From Adam we receive our human nature, from Christ the right and fact of participation in the divine nature.

The human race, the whole of creation too, has the God-man as its absolute and eternal Head. We are one body by, in and through him. We are his members. Marriage is the most obvious figure of his union with us as a race and as individuals. As in marriage the persons of husband and wife remain separate and yet are in a oneness of body through the consummation of the marriage act, so too is mankind the bride of Christ.

It is wrong to consider Redemption as merely the removal of guilt. It is that but far more. Christ died to deliver us from sin. In the words of the Creed, he became man "because of us men and our salvation". But the sacrifice of the Cross, extended, perpetuated, re-presented in the sacrifice-sacrament of the Holy Eucharist, not only frees us from sin but also admits us into the fellowship of the Trinity. "I have come that they may have life and have it more abundantly."

It is also wrong to consider Christ's "emptying" of himself as being his assumption of human nature. The Godhead could suffer no loss of glory by the Incarnation. The "emptying" implies that our Lord, of his own will, withheld from himself some of the gifts of integrity to which his human nature was entitled by reason of its union with his divine nature. He became as a "servant". He accepted the humble lot of Adam after the Fall. He knew hunger, pain, suffering and death, and "by his stripes we are healed". The way of suffering was not the only one by which redemption could have been achieved, but it was the way Christ chose, not only because he thus became like us and could bear our sorrows "in his body on the tree", not only because he gave us an example to follow, but above all, because by this complete and utter abasement he offered to the Father the worship and adoration of mankind from the depths to which sin had condemned us. It is for this that the Church calls Adam's sin a "happy" one, for from within the state resulting from our enmity with God, Christ worked our salvation and gave to the Father the perfect worship of the man-God at the Last Supper, in the agony of Gethsemani, through the death of the Cross.

As Scheeben puts it, Christ is the centre of gravity of the whole world-order. He draws all things to himself through his members in whom his sacred humanity lives on upon the earth. The sacramental life of the Church is nothing but this sacred humanity remaining with us, working among us and for us, using material things, water, oil, bread, wine, words, our bodies, our sexuality in marriage.

The Christian cannot separate sex from marriage. For him marriage consecrates man and woman for a special office, a special work in and for the mystical body, an office and work made possible by their sexuality and through which their sexuality becomes an instrument of divine grace. The marriage union, the oneness of the partners is, since the Redemption, a sacramental, supernatural state. Once again our animal nature has been raised into the realm of the divine. Through our sexuality thus sanctified, power flows from Christ our Head into the married couple.

Christians rightly argue that nature, apart from revelation, indicates a morality of sex. The biological purpose of marriage is obvious. The birth and education of children require an ethic, a code of love. Otherwise sexuality will run wild and threaten the race with personal and social disintegration. The work of generation is so noble that we may well found a natural morality upon its demands and implications. Valid though this argument is, it must be completed by the truth that grace perfects nature. Of itself, the argument from nature has two drawbacks. Under the Old Law, the unity and indissolubility of marriage—both of which seem to follow from the function of generation and marriage—were not insisted upon. The coming of Christ alone has made absolute the implied obligations of marriage but for reasons far more fundamental even than those implied in the duties of parenthood. Further, the immense importance Christianity attaches to the individual person raises the problem of the relation of sexuality to love. Many modern thinkers protest that to subordinate the love of man and wife to an impersonal, biological task, however noble in itself, is to reduce human personality to the level of an instrument. This is a powerful argument and, although it can be challenged on purely natural grounds by a thorough analysis of human love, yet, from the standpoint of Christian doctrine, the objection is met by showing the vital distinction between an instrument and an organ. Man and wife, even from a natural point of view, are not just passive instruments of a life-force, mere means to generation. They bring into the world new images of God and God himself infuses the human soul directly into each child. The married are therefore organs of his creative power. Even at the natural level they are co-workers with him "whom to serve is perfect freedom". Every marriage is holy in so far as the partners are called to this creative vocation. In the opening chapters of Genesis the fundamental principle is laid down by God: "What God, then, has joined, let not man put asunder" (Matt. 19. 6).

It is true that God did not insist always upon the full keeping of this law. It was only at the Incarnation that the obligation and the grace needed to fulfil it were restored to man. Yet, though the hardness of men's hearts made it impossible in many cases for the law to be obeyed, the root of marriage remained the same, waiting for the coming of Christ in order to grow again in the soil of grace. It is not therefore surprising that in all civilizations and at all times, marriage ceremonies included an oath of mutual fidelity and the invocation of the gods.

This natural union issuing from the creative will of God receives a sacramental character when husband and wife are already raised in baptism to a supernatural status. The purposes of their marriage then become themselves supernatural. Since the Incarnation, all mankind is potentially in this supernatural status. Christians are in it actually and their married union makes them organs of the mystical body. The Christian can only dispose of his soul and body as a member of Christ. St Paul makes this clear when he warns his converts that to lie with a harlot is to unite a member of Christ with a member of sin. The sexuality of the redeemed is to be an organ of the union of Christ and the Church and to bring into the world new members of Christ.

When this fact is pointed out, many feel that the physical acts of sexual union are in some way made to appear unclean. Nothing could be further from the truth. It is the consummation of the marriage which is the seal of the union of the partners. It is an image of the union of Christ and the Church. It is made holy and linked with Christ's union with his Church because the Christian man and wife are holy, sanctified by their baptism and members of the God-man. They are called to use their sexuality for the increase of the mystical body. The Catholic ethic of marriage stems from this primary fact. Scheeben sums up the

situation in words which should be known to every
Christian:

> Christian marriage . . . has a real, essential and intrinsic
> reference to the mystery of Christ's union with his Church.
> It is rooted in this mystery and is organically connected with
> it, and so partakes of its nature and mysterious character.
> Christian marriage is not simply a symbol of this mystery
> or a type that lies outside it, but an image growing out of
> the union of Christ with the Church and pervaded by it.
> For it not only symbolizes the mystery but really represents
> it. It represents the mystery because the mystery proves
> active and operative in it. (Scheeben, *op. cit.*, p. 606.)

We are familiar with the word "represents" in connection with the sacrifice of the Mass, which represents the
sacrifice of the Cross. This re-presentation is not merely
a commemoration, a representation in the ordinary sense,
it is the same sacrifice *presented again* in a sacramental
form. Must we believe then that, as Christ's body and
blood are truly present and offered in the Mass to the
Father, so too is his union with the Church really present
in the union of man and wife in Christian marriage? Yes,
provided that we realize that our Lord is physically and
in his substance present in the Eucharist, while in marriage
his presence as united to his Church is one of power and
grace only. The Christian man and wife are, in a limited
but true sense, an image of the still more intimate union
of Christ with mankind in the Eucharist.

The sacraments operate by the power of Christ their
source. It is true that their effect may be hindered by the
lack of the right disposition in those who receive them, but
their power and grace do not in themselves depend on the
good will of the recipient. They come from our Lord. We
may hinder grace, we cannot produce it. This is an important distinction in the case of every sacrament and especially
in that of marriage. We may fall into the error of thinking

that grace is not at work in us because we are not conscious of it, because we do not feel any emotional satisfaction when we receive a sacrament. Emotions have their place in human life and are by no means always absent from religious experience. But they are not essential to the latter. The supernatural life is above, below and beyond the natural life and our natural experiences are wholly inadequate to give us the awareness of the operation of grace in us. As the facts of the Christian faith are only certainly known through revelation, so too the presence and work of grace within us can only be truly known by faith.

The importance of this fact for the Christian man and wife is obvious. Any attempt to "feel" the sacramental reality in the actual sex life leads nowhere and may cause grave misunderstandings between the partners. Sacramental grace is present in their union and as such cannot be an object of feeling. Yet husband and wife must love one another not only with a natural but also with a supernatural love. They must, that is, remember always that for married Christians, their love is called to bring into being new members of Christ. Scheeben ends his chapter on Christian marriage with these words—

> Christian marriage is inextricably woven into the supernatural fabric of the Church; the greatest damage one can inflict on both is to tear them apart.... Nowhere does the mystical life of the Church penetrate more deeply into natural relationships.... Nowhere has the truth come more strikingly to light that the whole of nature, down to its deepest roots, shares in the sublime consecration of the God-man, who has taken this nature to himself. Nowhere does the truth more clearly appear that Christ has been made the cornerstone upon which God has based the preservation and growth of nature....
>
> [Christian matrimony] is a mystery that has its foundation in the wonderful works of the Incarnation and the Eucharist, and so alone can reveal their rich significance. (Scheeben, *op. cit.*, p. 610.)

This final sentence may startle us. Not even Christians are accustomed to look upon marriage as the sole means by which the rich significance of the Incarnation and the Eucharist are revealed. They fail, that is, to realize what is meant by the union of God and man in Christ. The union of the partners in Christian marriage contains in a true sense this union of God with man in Christ or rather is contained in it. Christian marriage is a supernatural union founded on the Incarnation. It reveals the divine humanity in so far as the married couple are visible organs of the divine humanity in their love and their fruitfulness. Their union of soul and body reveals the inner glory of the Eucharist since in this greatest of sacraments man is united to his Creator in body and in spirit, even as the body and soul of husband and wife are made one in marriage.

The Christian approach to the facts of sex is determined by these spiritual, supernatural realities. Sexuality for the Christian has been assumed whole and entire into the infinite scope of the Incarnation. Its natural function is made subordinate to, included in the organism of the Church as the Bride of Christ. Sexuality in marriage is consecrated to the divine work of the Redemption. To use it as though it had not been redeemed is to deny to it the grace and glory it has received from Christ's restoration of the fullness of its meaning. Sexuality and the divine humanity are joined together and for man to put them asunder is to blaspheme the God-man. To give rein to sexual passions outside marriage is to destroy the work of Christ.

This may seem an austere and negative doctrine when we experience the great movements of physical desire which sweep across the soul. Like the apostles, we may cry out "Who then shall be saved?" The answer is simply: those who love, for love is the force through which sexuality in man is to be controlled and directed. To love we must turn if we are fully to understand the rôle of our sexuality in human life as the Christian sees it.

In Shakespeare's *Twelfth Night* there is a song of which the second verse runs——

> What is love, 'tis not hereafter,
> Present mirth hath present laughter,
> What's to come is still unsure . . .

In St Paul's letter to the Corinthians we read: "The time will come when we shall outgrow prophecy, when speaking with tongues will come to an end, when knowledge will be swept away: love will never fail" (1 Cor. 13. 8). To the pleasure-seeker, the sceptic, the materialist, love—whatever its origin and cause—is "not hereafter", it will pass away; nothingness is the ultimate reality. If there is mirth, its laughter will die and with it the love which gave it birth. For the Christian, for any man who believes in realities which will never fail, love is a window open on to eternity. It is the gateway to the kingdom of the abiding.

The needs of the child require that its parents remain united not only under the same roof but also in mutual love. We know that the healthy mental and physical development of the child demands not only that it should be loved by its parents but also that it should be aware that its parents love one another. The natural structure of the family implies a permanent love. Love which leads to sexual union is not the only form of this transcendent force, there is the love of friendship, which is found both in the married union and in the mutual affection and service which bind men together. In its highest form it leads to the complete sacrifice of life for the person loved. "This is the greatest love a man can shew," said our Lord, "that he should lay down his life for his friends" (John 15. 13).

For sexual love the issue is simply this: is the love of man and woman to be only temporary, bound up entirely

with the generative and educative duties of parenthood, or
does it include a love which will endure throughout life
making any sexual union with others impossible? Marriage
as a natural union already has a kind of pre-sacramental
character and normally includes an oath of fidelity and
the invocation of the gods. In the Christian sacrament there
is a contract of fidelity, a promise of perseverance, "for
better, for worse; for richer, for poorer; in sickness and in
health; till death do us part".

For some thinkers, the demands of human love are so
sacred and so personal that they separate it from the biological function of generation. For them, this racial task
cannot determine the love of persons. Had Christ not become man, this argument would be difficult to rebut. Since
the Incarnation, it cannot stand. Human love in our fallen
state moves between the opposing poles of Law and freedom. It is only when God, who is love, becomes man and
assumes human love into the love of the Spirit for the
Father and the Son, that Law becomes the way in which
love works out its purposes, and freedom no longer opens
the way to chaos.

Married love stemming now from the love of Christ for
men takes the biological law and the technique of sexual
love into itself and sanctifies them. The married couple
united by the Christian sacrament have become the image
of the love of the God-man for the human race, of that
love which will never fail. Divorce is as absurd for them
and as inconceivable as the thought of Christ casting away
the race to which he is eternally wedded.

An idealistic dream, we may mutter. You may forbid
divorce, you cannot stop love from dying, it can and it
does. Life together becomes a torment. How can you insist
that it continue in the name of love, human or divine? We
shall face this problem in a later chapter. For the moment,
we merely indicate the lines of a solution. Our Lord was

entitled by his divine humanity to be free from all suffering. He abandoned that title and redeemed us through
suffering and death. His love for the Father and for us
was made manifest in his agony and on the Cross. As
Pascal says, Christ will suffer till the end of time. He will
suffer in us, his members. We are not directly conscious
either of grace or of the supernatural value of our suffering. We are made like Christ "the suffering servant", the
"man of sorrows and acquainted with grief", so that we
may ultimately share in his risen glory. The married cannot be exempt from suffering, and the love which is the
heart of their union may be subjected to almost intolerable
strain and tension. To seek relief in divorce is to refuse the
Cross. There are circumstances, we must admit, in which
divorce seems the only way out of an impossible situation.
Yet the Christian cannot believe any such situation is ever
completely impossible.

For the time being, we state categorically that one of the
noblest projects of the race—the subordination of the
sexual passions to love and to generation through love—
has been approved, ratified, consecrated, assumed into the
union of Christ with mankind. To allow divorce is to deny
to marriage its place as an organ of Christ's mystical body
and as the image of his eternal union with men.

At this point, Catholics who have not hitherto been
aware of the fullness of the Church's doctrine of marriage
may meet another and different problem. If, they may say,
marriage is a sacrament of the Church and the image of
Christ's union with it, why must we believe that consecrated virginity is a higher state? This is not an academic
question, it expresses a genuine difficulty. At the present
time, the theology of marriage is in process of development
and we may be tempted to think that the traditional teaching on the vow of chastity is bound up with an outmoded
and puritanical idea of sex. This is not so. Both marriage

and consecrated virginity reveal the truth concerning the
place of sex in the Christian life. An analysis of the purpose of the vow of chastity throws light on the character
of Christian marriage, while, as Guitton points out so
forcibly in his *Essay on Human Love,* a study of the
realities involved in marriage helps us to understand why
the Church holds consecrated virginity to be the higher
state.

Two statements must be made at the outset. The first
has already been brought forward in a former quotation
from Scheeben, "Christian matrimony has its foundation
in the wonderful works of the Incarnation and the Eucharist, and so alone can reveal their true significance." The
second, again a quotation from Scheeben, reads: "By taking religious vows ... the member of the Church is more
closely wedded to Christ, and so expresses more directly
the relation of the Church to Christ, than is the case in
matrimony. Nevertheless, the pronouncing of religious
vows is not a sacramental act: it is an act of subjective,
personal dedication, and merits grace only *ex opere
operantis*."[1] Scheeben seems to be contradicting himself.
If marriage alone reveals the full meaning of the Incarnation and the Eucharist, how can the taking of the vows
express more directly the relation of Christ and the
Church?

We must ask what it is that the Christian does when he
takes the vow of chastity. He promises to abstain from
every kind of sexual activity. He seems to affirm by this
act that marriage would prevent him from the perfect union
with Christ to which he believes he is called. As Scheeben
says, the vow weds him more closely to Christ than would
marriage. Why? St Paul has the answer. He it is who has
given us the most profound theology of Christian marriage
and his advice to the married in his letter to the Ephesians

[1] *Op. cit.,* footnote to p. 605.

is the source of much subsequent teaching on matrimony. Yet it is he who preaches the superiority of virginity, and for a reason which at first sight seems trivial. A married man, he says, thinks how he may please his wife, a man who has taken the vow of chastity is free to think only of the service of God. The triviality is only apparent. It contains a profound truth. In modern terms, the married state is rooted in a whole complex of biological, psychological, sociological realities, in a whole web of circumstance and under the force of laws over which the married can exercise little control or choice. The consecrated virgin is free to follow the dictates of the Spirit in ways impossible to the married who must, for it is their vocation, manifest the union of Christ and the Church in and through the pattern of life which their state involves. And this pattern is largely determined for them by law and custom.

But there is more in St Paul's dictum. Virginity is not a denial of sexuality or a turning away from it. It consecrates it. So too does marriage. In each case there is a different purpose and vital structure. The consecration is achieved by the married in their sacramental union, and in the case of the Christian who takes the vow of chastity, through a personal dedication which does not and cannot have the status of a sacrament. The married couple is an organ of the mystical body, officially designated and empowered to beget and rear new beings for the Kingdom of God. Its apostolic mission is to shew forth in its community life and fruitfulness the union of God and man in Christ. This implies a renunciation of all use of sexuality outside of marriage and of all illegitimate use of it in marriage. Sacrifice is at the heart of marriage, for marriage demands an oblation, an offering of self. The marriage vow is made to the partner. Man and wife are consecrated to God's service not directly but through each other. The consecrated virgin makes a complete renouncement of genital sexuality; even its legitimate use in marriage is forgone. This is not done out of any fear of sexuality as such, or because of some Manichean horror of sex as material or evil. Our Lord himself taught the real purpose of the virginal state when he said that some become "eunuchs" for the sake of the Kingdom of God. It is a question then of a greater by contrast with a lesser good.

How then does the vow of chastity express more directly than the sacrament of matrimony the union of Christ and the Church? The answer surely lies in the fact that as Christ withheld from his human nature the full gifts of human integrity to which he was entitled, so we too must make the same renunciation, redeemed though we are by and in him, and equally entitled with him to the complete integrity of Adam before the Fall. Virginity in Eden had no merit. Passion was under the control of reason. Not so in us, redeemed though we are. Our Lord could not experience this upsurge of passion; all other human anguish and suffering he endured and infinitely more intensely than we can ever do. When St Paul says, however, that we are to make up for what is lacking in the sufferings of Christ, it is not too fanciful to believe that he had partly in mind those storms of passion with which we have so often to contend. The married know how hard it is to protect their marriage from self-seeking. It is no news to anyone that sex is a source of misery, crime, sordid calculation, lust and tragedy of every sort. Not because it is evil, but since man though redeemed has still to undergo the constant attack of disordered passions. The grace of the sacrament of matrimony is there to enable those who use it honestly to ride the storm and, in their married lives, to make sexuality what it is destined to be, the servant of their love of God and of one another. But the price is suffering.

The consecrated virgin has renounced the state of marriage and the strains and stresses which are inevitably bound up with it. The passions are not thereby quiescent in him. He has undertaken a still more difficult struggle. The married have ample opportunity in their work as parents, to subdue the urges of passion to the real tasks of reason and will. The virgin forgoes the comforts and helps of family life as well as its troubles and tumult. He has to show forth the union of Christ and the Church *as it will essentially be in the Kingdom of the Resurrection.* In heaven there is no giving in marriage. The body will be wholly occupied in the worship and contemplation of God. In a sense, then, the monk and nun image the transfigured Christ of Thabor, the Christ of glory, the Bridegroom of the Church in the eternal freedom of a fully integrated humanity. This they can do only imperfectly and by a personal dedication which of its very nature cannot be sacramental, for sacraments are concerned with the this-world presence and work of Christ. To the virginal vocation few are called and these make an oblation of self to Christ and also to his members, especially to those who are consecrated to him in matrimony.

They reveal to the married the essence of their own marital union. That essence is itself truly virginal. Christ has assumed into his mystical body the processes of generation, but these and the sacrament which consecrates them, will pass away in the world to come. Only love, pure and out-going to the Father, the Son and the Spirit, and to all the members of the mystical body, will remain for ever and ever. Already in this life, this pure love is the ideal of the married, who are to strive after it in their relations to one another, to their children and to all other men and women. Already in this life, the consecrated virgins, by their renunciation of the joys and sorrows of married life, show—in so far as their lives correspond with the high ideal to which they are wedded—the utter unselfishness of love, the virginal heart too of marriage, which our fallen though redeemed nature finds so hard to see at the very centre of our married life.

The mysteries of love and generation are nowhere more clearly revealed than in the virginal motherhood of our Lady. The doctrine we have outlined implies the fact of her immaculate conception. By the overshadowing of the Creator Spirit she conceived the Second Person of the Blessed Trinity according to his human nature. The infinite honour thus done to mankind must be understood. Woman in the person of our Lady brings forth the God-man as the fruit of a divine and perfect love, the love of the Spirit. In return her love for the Father and the Spirit had to be pure from all self-seeking, all self-regarding passion. By her immaculate conception, the forces of human passion were prevented from setting up their strife in her soul. She was preserved from original sin by the merits of the sacrifice of Christ which was to come. In the Church, those called to consecrated virginity image the perfect love of Mary for God, expressed in her answer to the angel: "Behold the handmaid of the Lord, let it be unto me according to thy word." In the Church, the married image her fruitfulness in their own child-bearing. The religious and the married are complementary. Both make a sacrifice of their own bodies, but that of the religious is greater since by it he indicates that total direct surrender of body and soul which all will make in the life to come. He thus shows to the married the inner meaning and the ultimate goal of their own union. He offers them an example of what supernatural love involves, what it is prepared to do, and thus makes it easier for them to strive to make their own love for one another more pure, more like that of Christ for the Church. By giving himself wholly to the Church and her work, he shows the Christian husband how he too in his own consecrated sacramental task may love his wife as Christ loved the Church and gave himself for it.

On the other hand, the married reveal to the religious the fruitfulness of love. They are always a challenge to him. His own life has its temptations, none the less tragic for being more subtle, less crude and obvious than those which face the married. He may become sterile in his love for Christ. His is the temptation of the Pharisee, to glory in good works. He too must bear fruit in the lives of others as do the married in the lives of their children. Whether in an active or contemplative religious life, the call is always essentially the same—to be one with Christ in his redeeming love for mankind. And the heart of this love of Christ for the race is his love for his Father. We shall be Christ's and he will offer us all and forever to the Father.

Religious and the married, each in their own degree of oblation, of self-sacrifice, foreshadow that great day of final revelation and everlasting glory.

# PART II

# THE FACTS OF THE PRESENT SITUATION

CHAPTER IV

# SEX AND THE BODY

The previous chapters may have convinced the reader that this book is only one more example of the abstract preaching which is so wearisome and meaningless to those daily embroiled in sexual passions and the options they raise. Granted that what has been said is true, how can it be related to this continual struggle? And may it not, after all, be only a learned way of clothing irrational taboos in theological dress?

We shall not meet this objection directly. Instead we shall turn at the beginning of this section to the Kinsey Reports on Sexual Behaviour in the Human Male and the Human Female. It seems a far cry from dogmatic theology to the facts recorded by Kinsey and his colleagues. However subject to criticism and modification the statistics they set out may prove to be, the fact remains that the extent to which men and women of every social rank, profession, religious persuasion, behave sexually in ways which the Christian is obliged to call objectively sinful, is far greater than we imagined. We do not know what moral presuppositions were in the minds of Kinsey and his assistants when they began their researches. They had rightly resolved to be completely scientific, to record what they discovered. This however did not prevent them from making comments of a general and even controversial nature. They have a right to do this, particularly if their discoveries appear to warrant interpretation. One observation of Kinsey's is especially important. He suggests that no moral theory of sexual behaviour is valid or likely to have practical results if it bases itself on taboos, sociological custom, law or religious doctrine. These, he says, have all been tried and have signally failed to modify appreciably the patterns of sexual behaviour.

It would not be unfair to claim that Kinsey has one axiom—sexual conduct is the outcome of stimulus. Man is an animal. His neurological structure is conditioned to respond automatically to stimuli. No ethical system can succeed in practice if it does not take this primary fact into account. Man is related to the primates. What are called sexual "aberrations" are merely mammalian behaviour patterns which naturally and inevitably are found in man. To condemn them is to close one's eyes to the realities of man's ancestry, to the physical facts of his bodily existence. Masturbation, pre-marital petting, pre-marital and extra-marital intercourse are all much more common than was believed. In view of our animal nature, this is not surprising.

We may not argue, says Kinsey, that sexual "abnormalities" are the cause of neurotic symptoms or of psychosis. People who become neurotic after behaviour commonly thought to be sinful, do so not as a direct result of such behaviour, but because they are suffering from a mental conflict induced by social taboos upon that behaviour. Primitive peoples who do not have these taboos offer no evidence of neurosis caused by what the Judeo-Christian codes hold to be immoral practices.

Kinsey's honest statement of his views, his challenge to the moralist are to be welcomed and met with equal honesty. The patron of the Christian sexologist is not the ostrich. Had we been content to expand our own first three chapters into a whole book and to leave it at that, we should have done a disservice to the reader. Kinsey himself obviously had second thoughts. He writes: "These data (on extra-marital intercourse) emphasize the fact that the reconciliation of the married individual's desire for coitus with a variety of sexual partners, and the maintenance of a stable marriage, presents a problem which has not been satisfactorily resolved in our culture. It is not likely to be resolved until *man moves more completely away from his mammalian ancestry*" (Sexual Behaviour in the Human Female, p. 436, our italics).

Christianity does not teach a sexual ethic distinct from a rational human morality. It holds that there is a natural moral law valid for all men, whether Christians or not. The only specifically Christian articles in the Church's sexual code are the prohibition of divorce and the theology of marriage as a sacrament. Even here, the sacrament is not something other than the natural contract but the contract itself raised to the supernatural status of a sacrament. Nor is the Church's prohibition of divorce applicable only to sacramental marriage. It is a restatement, in Christ's name, of the indissolubility of *all* valid unions.

We admit that this ethic is often presented as a series of taboos, a list of prohibitions. On the other hand, it is significant that Kinsey can produce two large volumes on sexual behaviour in which the word "love" rarely appears. Christians should not cast the first stone at him. There is little talk of love in our own statements of sexual morality. And to leave out or minimize love in this connection is to reduce morality to taboo. Yet Kinsey is not entirely blameless here. For him, what he calls the "mores", that is, the theoretical sexual laws of the society in which a man lives, largely determine the pattern of conscience if not of behaviour. He fails to see that he is himself creating new "mores" with new taboos as their bases—all that is not a scientific fact objectively observed is irrelevant: the moralist must build on this foundation and seek ways and means of leading men to a stage of evolution more removed from that of the mammalian genus to which he belongs.

In a word, Kinsey and those who think with him, confuse two distinct trends in evolution. In terms of physiology, they concentrate on the vegetative, diencephalic constituents of human nature and forget or reduce the rational and emotional elements as they are represented in the enormous development of the cerebral pallium. Canon Masure has a profound observation on this type of thinking, although his terms of reference are wider. There has been a confusion, he says, between the order of the development of human thought and the order of the evolution of the different stages of creation. Living things have evolved from the simple to the complex. Human thought has developed in an opposite direction. It was at first satisfied with a theodicy. It then worked out a philosophy and finally a science. Briefly, organic evolution has proceeded to a synthesis, while human thought has moved to an ever greater degree of analysis. We may note that a similar phenomenon is observable in our individual growth. We pass from simple acceptance to a stage of philosophical inquiry. The child puts the ultimate metaphysical question: Why? We then move to the knowledge of details. Unfortunately, as Masure insists, thinkers tend to argue backwards. Thought, they claim, must now evolve organically from the simple notions to an eventual synthesis founded on the pattern of organic evolution. It is this mistake which lies at the back of the minds of those who hold with Kinsey that we must base our sexual ethic on mammalian behaviour patterns.

The truth is surely very different. What Kinsey asks us

to do, the process of evolution has already done for us.[1]
The whole sexual problem is for man at a different level.
Otherwise neither Kinsey nor his readers would be bother-
ing their heads about the rights and wrongs of sexuality.

To return for a moment to Masure. The first phenomena
of creation, he says, seem to have been those of physics and
under the rule of the laws of attraction and weight. Chemical reactions then followed and gave rise to living organisms, plants, fixed to the soil by roots, and then to freely
moving organisms. With man we reach the sphere of the
psychological and moral consciousness. He has memory
and intelligence. The problem of his destiny sets him in
the sphere of religion where his natural powers are inadequate. He thirsts for mystery, because he thirsts for
God. God takes him by the hand. Man passes beyond himself into the realm of the supernatural.[2]

For the Christian, therefore, the problems of sexual
morality cannot be appraised only by reference to a former
stage of human evolution. The facts of consciousness and
of intelligence have brought new states of existence into
the animal world and each new state has its own particular
ends, purposes, obligations, rights and duties inherent in
the sphere of life to which it gives man access. This does
not mean that the former states have passed completely
away. On the contrary, they remain, but as assumed into
the higher states which have succeeded them in time. Man
is a mammal but a mammal with a difference. None of

[1] We wish to make it clear that in the pages which follow we do
not assume that the theory of organic evolution in the case of man
has been *proved*. We are arguing with our opponents on their own
chosen ground. This does not imply an uncritical acceptance of
their postulates which, in the Church's view, it is imprudent to
consider as certain. Future scientific discovery may modify this
view in either direction.

[2] In *Le Coupable est-il un malade ou un pécheur?*, pp. 174, 175,
Spes, Paris, 1951.

his behaviour problems, sexual or otherwise, can be solved apart from his mammalian structures—Kinsey is right there—but neither can they be solved solely in terms of those structures. A moral synthesis must be as complex as is man himself, man mammal, man intelligent, man conscious, man social, man political, man emotional, man passive, man active, man the son of God.

The Christian too must not try to simplify what is complex. He must not attempt to acquire at one jump by his own strength the simplicity of God in whom alone all things are one, as in their beginning and last end. There can be no such simplicity for man until he sees all things at one in God in the Beatific Vision.

For the Christian there is the temptation to leap to a false simplicity, a simple, self-chosen gesture of the mind which it is imagined will solve all the manifold human problems. The desire for such a simple and radical solution is sound and the solution in fact exists although its simplicity is only apparent. It is the life of love. The Christian must not make *à rebours* the mistake which distorts Kinsey's thought. He must not try to think of, contemplate and practise love apart from all the complex vegetative, animal, physiological, rational, psychological structure of his nature. He must see *all* the facts and in a hierarchical order of value. He must not consider the lower levels of human nature as without value or relevance, as having been superseded by instead of assumed into the rational consciousness. Christ has drawn all things to himself. We must not transfer the sense of guilt due to original sin to the physical and psychological characteristics God has given us. If we do we shall fall into the trap which lies in the path of the scientific investigator. Those who insist on man's physical links with the other mammals as the sole or principal source of his sexual behaviour close their eyes to his other characteristics. They assume too that the

previous stages of his mental development are now irrelevant, that theology and philosophy are outmoded, that a
new synthesis must be built on the basis of scientific
observation. This would be sound practice if the scale of
values in the evolution of mind were parallel to those in
the evolution of the body. This is not so. In fact science
autonomous in its own field depends for its ultimate value
upon metaphysical fact, while philosophy, again autonomous in its proper sphere, depends ultimately for its
value upon the fact of God's existence and nature. And of
God's *nature*, as St Thomas says, we can discover only
what he is not. Revelation alone can speak positively in
that absolute realm of knowledge.

One obvious fact is always to be borne in mind: since
man is conscious, his present evolution is within his own
control, it is his own affair. Rationality opens the way to
truth and is the mother of insight. As Solovyev says:
"Comparing his actions with this higher knowledge man
may infinitely improve his existence and nature, *without
departing from the boundaries of human forms*."[3] Love is
the realm in which this further evolution takes place. Of
all the forms of love, sexual love is particularly important
since it includes all the mammalian bases and assumes
them into its own outward and upward movement towards
unity with the universe, with mankind, with God.

Solovyev points out that the whole process of evolution
is the story of success after repeated failure. It is unrealistic
to argue that since love has failed in the past it must inevitably do so in the future. Yet we have to remember that
while rational consciousness has developed *in* but not
*through* man, the highest stage of his evolution, that is,
the life of love, has come and must continue to come
*through* man's own conscious effort.

[3] Solovyev, *The Meaning of Love*, English translation by Jane
Marshall, Geoffrey Bles, 1945, p. 18.

Our own individual and personal evolution presents us with this challenge. In childhood we reach consciousness and rationality, but if we are to become true persons, centres of liberty and choice, vehicles of an ever widening and increasingly higher form of human existence, if we are to become individually and racially what we have it in us to become, then we must pass beyond the state of individual egoism, where we tend to see ourselves as the only centre of experience and meaning. We shall only truly find ourselves, as Christ has taught us, by losing ourselves. Sexual love is not the only form of love but it affords for the vast majority of men and women a signal opportunity for this life-giving death to self and in a most dynamic and insistent form. Our sexual behaviour may either reverse the process of racial and individual evolution or carry it forward. Our sexuality presents us with this alternative, this inescapable choice.

For the Christian the call to love is not only a fact of nature but a vocation in grace. He is commanded to love his wife and to give himself for her as Christ loved and gave himself for the Church. He is to be the saviour of his wife in so far as by his love for her—spiritual and physical—he promotes the full growth of her personality in and through their mutual love. Sexual love achieves this total union of two persons at far deeper levels than does the love of friendship since it includes the whole of a man's and a woman's nature, the complete bodily, rational and spiritual being of both. Our Lord's saying "Strait is the gate and narrow is the way" is verified in the married vocation. "The individual's desire for coitus with a variety of sexual partners" of which Kinsey writes, is the expression of a dispersal of vital and spiritual energy. Beyond the physical pleasure or the passing emotion lies the desire for personal growth, for salvation in the psychological sense of the finding of one's oneself, the discovery of a centre for the whole complex structure of one's psycho-physical being. The movement towards others is sound. There lies the way, but to flit from one partner to another in fact drives a man back into his own ego. Rational consciousness survives because during our lives we each find some pattern of permanence. A constant dispersal of mental energy in unrelated activities eventually brings breakdown and a threat to self-consciousness and mental balance. Sexual promiscuity hinders the forward leap of the personality into that freedom from isolated individuality which alone brings us to full adult structure. As Solovyev has written:

> Only under the action of this, so to speak, chemical fusion of two creatures, of the same nature and of equal significance, *but on all sides* distinct as to form, is the creation possible (both in the idea of Nature and in the spiritual order) of a new man, the actual realization of an authentic human individuality. Such a fusion, or at least a close approximation to it, we find in sex-love, for which reason we attach to it exceptional importance.... (*Op. cit.*, p. 26, author's italics.)

The operative word here is "love". We must distinguish between the sexual *instinct*, which, as Kinsey rightly insists, responds automatically to stimuli, and sexual *love*, which controls the reactions to them in the interests of higher purposes and yet both includes and transcends them.

We may ask why sexual behaviour should be singled out for special treatment, why it is taken for granted that we transcend our mammalian structures in other aspects of life while we remain at a purely animal stage in our sex life. It is obvious that many prefer this to be the case. There are also those who give their aggressive instincts full play—the flick knife is symbolic of a whole attitude to life. We may doubt whether a scientific consideration of its anti-social uses would force us to conclude that the stimuli to aggression being always present we must refer the whole matter to our mammalian ancestry whose patterns the delinquent is merely preserving. The truth is that the general social milieu moves certain individuals towards more primitive and irrational conduct. The solution of their problem lies in the emergence of a higher social conscience.

The analogy with sexuality is imperfect yet the principle, that is, that we cannot argue from stimuli to ethics, is valid in both cases. Human sexual intercourse is not just the contact of two bodies. The personal, emotional, psychological, spiritual realities cannot be separated from it. They may be repressed or treated as taboos, but they will continue to be present and to influence our sexual relations. Kinsey has anticipated an objection of this kind. He forestalls it by stating: "Those aspects of behaviour which we identify as psychologic can be *nothing but* certain aspects of that same basic anatomy and physiology" (*op. cit.*, p. 646, our italics).

This is a curious dogma. It implies that the evolutionary process, as far as human psychology is concerned, has not brought man to a new realm of existence and experience, but has merely given a "new look" to his anatomical and physiological characteristics. If this is so, evolution is no more than a mere change in appearances, while the substantial reality of physical beings remains unchanged. Presumably, other stages of evolution—the mind, reason, art, thought, science itself—cannot claim exemption from this restrictive interpretation. The cathedrals, the philosophies, Bach's B minor Mass, atomic physics, are all no more than manifestations of human biology and physiology. That they are inseparable from the body is obvious. That they are only extensions of the bodily structure is a dogma requiring an act of faith far more naked and unsupported than the Christian makes in accepting the articles of the Creed.

There is a distinction between spirit and life, between the vital and the intelligent phenomena of human experience.

A genuine sexual ethic will neither neglect nor misinterpret this distinction. If man is totally included in his anatomical, physiological structure then science itself and Dr Kinsey's researches are only reactions to stimuli in the physical order and have no further reference. This is surely a denial of any real meaning to the word "evolution". As Masure writes: "The idea of defining beings not as they are or now ought to be, but by what God could one day make them if he so wishes or wished, seems like non-Euclidean geometry, a strange, incoherent project. Yet it is one of the Christian visions of man and perhaps of the universe" (*op. cit.*, p. 169). God is the origin and goal of all creatures. In a true sense he brings the greater from the less. Morality therefore does not judge acts as though they were static, it considers their direction and their future consequences.

The distinction between spirit and life is most important. By "life" in this context we mean the forces of preservation and reproduction which drive living organisms to the search for food, for sexual union and to all the other requisites of physical survival and generation. It would be a gross misreading of Christian doctrine to assume that by her insistence on child-bearing as the primary end of marriage, the Church is consecrating these vital forces at the expense of the spirit and of the love which is its deepest characteristic. It is regrettable that Christians have often given and still give the impression that this is so. Spirit and flesh, spirit and life cannot be separated in mankind, though they can and must be distinguished the one from the other in the Christian ethic. The Christian welcomes Scheler's dictum that true sexual love is vital and creative and that it is the expression of our desire to lead our lives at a level always higher than that of any given moment.[4]

The sexual acts have two ends, one vital and repro-

[4] In [Fr. trans.] *Nature et formes de la sympathie*, Paris, 1950.

ductive, the other, the expression and the full achievement of mutual love. These two purposes cannot be separated. God has joined man and woman not only as animals reproducing their species, but as two persons vowed to love. The sexual acts must be the outward expression of that love if they are to be human. The love itself must be creative, must inscribe itself upon the reproductive vital structure of the body or it is a parody of the love of pure spirits, a form of angelism.

Kinsey bluntly states the objection to the Christian doctrine. The Judeo-Christian code, he insists, holds all sexual acts to be unlawful except those which are directed to procreation. It refuses to recognize sexuality as a means to pleasure. But for the man and woman in the concrete situations of life, it is precisely this pleasure aspect which is uppermost. The Christian code attempts to force a doctrinaire pattern on an activity which will not and cannot receive it. The proof of the pudding ... the failure of Christianity to impose its sexual ethic even on its own followers!

Failure to achieve a purpose is not in itself proof that the purpose is illegitimate. As Solovyev points out, the evolutionary process has known failures enough but has not thereby ceased to drive living creatures forward to ultimate success. The point then is not whether the Christian ethic has achieved its purposes but whether this ethic is valid in itself, whether its claim to be the statement of a natural law is justified. This question is exercising the minds of Christian sexologists at the present time. They know that the progress of neurology, endocrinology, psychology, has a direct bearing on ethics. They are equally aware that the fact of love remains as the primal force inherent in all truly human relationships. Man must love God with his whole strength and his neighbour as himself. They see no reason why sexual relations which involve the whole man to a greater extent than any other type of union should be an exception to the law of love. They do not see why the expression of love in the context of a biological process—that of reproduction—should claim to override this law and put in its stead the pursuit of pleasure. That this is done so often does not make it any less a sin against nature and against love. They cannot approve of a man considering a woman as nothing more than a source of physical stimuli. This to them is a regression to a sub-human status. If the evolutionary process has in fact taken place, then the whole point about it is that by it we have *evolved*.

The future task of the Christian sexologist is to examine the neurological, endocrine and psychological data and to understand in the light of new knowledge what processes are involved in, what obstacles threaten, man's project of making sexual activity the expression of true love, and of finding in love the dynamism which will direct all responses to stimuli, all the physical phenomena of sexuality, all the emotional patterns of sexual experience towards an even fuller expression of love. To criticize the Christian sexual code as treating sexual intercourse solely as a mechanism of generation is a gross distortion of the facts.

The Christian for his part must beware of pretending that the extremely complex realities of sexuality are really simple. As Mgr Knox pointed out in a book which was still unfinished when he died, we "must portray the living Church not as a harassed official 'handing out' information at a press conference, but as a patient pioneer washing out the gold from the turbid stream of her own memories" (in *The Tablet* for March 28th, 1959). Nowhere is this more necessary than in the realm of sex. The sex problem is one of the most acute in our time; it offers the Christian a great opportunity. He must not think he has answered every question bv quoting Canon Law. Law is no substitute for theology, still less for love. The relevant articles in the Code are to be interpreted in the light of a theology and philosophy of love which we already possess, in the light too of a theology and philosophy of sexuality for which we are only now beginning to assemble the materials.

For this latter project we need the cooperation of scientists, philosophers, theologians, confessors, doctors, psychologists, married and unmarried members of the general public, of all in short who have daily to deal with the problems sexuality presents in their own lives and in those of others.

Kinsey's work, in spite of the reservations which have been made against some of his presuppositions and his statistical methods, is an honest and valid attempt to discover how people do in fact behave. It reveals the chaotic state of sexual activity among the American population. There is no reason to believe conditions are very much different elsewhere. Kinsey's two reports raise in an acute form the question of the definition of sexual "abnormality". Christians may learn from them to adopt a more sympathetic and objective attitude towards the difficulties of others.

Abbé Oraison has pointed out that in man sexuality seems to be on the threshold of a great revelation, of a vast realm in which love masters and perfects the physical automatism of animal instinct. Yet we find in fact a wide range of behaviour and innumerable levels of individual evolution. Some behave with little more responsibility than animals, others are choked with the weeds of irrational inhibitions which stifle their life forces, dam up the sources of their energy and favour the spindly growth of neuroses. In all our studies, teaching and, above all, in our own sex lives we are called to a task demanding continual generosity, a sure knowledge of the facts of faith and of sin, a true sense of the difference between sins due to false principles on the one hand and to human weakness on the other, a sense too of the distinction between formal and material sin. Above all, we need to have a love of others founded in true humility. We have our Lord's example. Who are we to throw the first stone, for who of us has not sinned against love? Yet both to ourselves and to others, we must repeat Christ's words: "Go and sin no more," at the same time doing all in our power to make it possible for the command to be obeyed.

We must not forget that Redemption "thus appears not as a price demanded for sin, but in a sense as a reward offered for sin itself, by bringing to fruition the natural desire which is at its root" (Abbé Rambaud in *Le Coupable est-il un malade ou un pécheur?* Paris, 1951, page 206). Beyond even the vilest sin we have to learn to see the good yearning of which it is the hideous caricature. In the problems and conditions love meets in its struggle for the mastery, we must learn to see not only the results of the Fall, but the hidden channels of grace which all suffering, pain and difficulty contain since Christ bore, and died upon, the cross which we too are bidden daily to carry.

# CHAPTER V

# SEX AND THE PSYCHE

At this point in the argument we meet the psychologist. He may protest that the last pages of the previous chapter are little more than mere exhortation. He is in daily contact with men and women whose lives are bedevilled by neuroses of which many, if not all, are either the result of an inadequate or distorted sexual development or are the causes of sexual difficulties when they are not their direct consequence. And one of the prime causes of neurotic suffering is the attempt to impose on sexuality a pattern derived from an abstract philosophy or theology. Men and women are not abstractions. Each has both the fundamental mental structure common to us all, and also his or her individual psyche whose growth has been influenced by others, by the family, the social class, the nation, the culture of the day and by a hundred other forces.

Further, the chief contribution of modern psychological research and theory to our knowledge is the discovery of the unconscious, that vast realm, personal and collective, which plays so significant and powerful a rôle in our conscious behaviour even if it does not wholly determine it. The very title of this book, we shall be told, begs the question. Who is this "Christian"? And what is this "sex"? We pass a host of Christians in the street. They will all perhaps subscribe to a list of abstract dogmas; they may all agree on moral principles—again in the abstract. Yet each is the product of far more than creed and code. One has the outlook of a primitive, another the psychological make-up of a generation still to come, another may be a mere cipher, a parrot with no personality of his own worth the name.

"Sex" too in the concrete has a multitude of resonances. To one it is a regrettable survival. All the theology in the world will not shake this radical and irrational conviction. To another it is an agonizing problem which his faith seems quite unable to solve. To a third it is the flowering of the whole personality, the great expression of love which we have said it is always destined to be, the image of the union of Christ and the Church not only in theory but also in fact.

All these Christians belong to different social classes and, as Kinsey has shown, there are considerable variations of sexual custom in the various strata of society, and custom has far more power than the abstract teaching of the theologian and philosopher. As he points out, marriage guidance counsellors rightly see the breakdown of many marriages as due to lack of sexual adjustment between the partners. The man is in a hurry. He thinks only of himself or is unable to control the rhythms of his sexual reactions. The woman is left unsatisfied; she has had no true orgasm. The couple are told to alter their ways. On the face of it, a sensible piece of advice! But if the code of the social class to which one or both belong considers all techniques of love-making as upper class perversions—and Kinsey claims that this is the common belief of the working class —then the woman will refuse to accept the suggestion even although her husband may be willing to try to carry it out. Even prostitutes of working class origin are loath to accept what they consider perverted attentions.

Nor will this be the end of the psychologist's objections. His justification is the casuistry dear to moral theologians.

Casuistry is a much maligned science. Priests who hear confessions are well aware of the bewildering complexity of men's personal problems. They will admit that when they give advice in addition to absolution, they cannot speak completely in the abstract. They too have their unconscious social bias, which, when they offer counsel may get in the way of fruitful communication with the penitent. It was to counter the procrustean application of inflexible law to individual cases that casuistry was invented.

Moral theologians know that their science too develops and must take account of any new knowledge bearing on human behaviour. As Oraison points out, a detailed knowledge of the neurophysical aspects of the sexual reflexes and of the way in which they are to be harmonized with the affective reactions, is necessary if we are to be able to define a complete and normal human sexuality.[1]

To publish a book on sexuality is therefore a risky business. What we say to others, they will inevitably interpret in the light of their own temperament and experience. However, there are facts which are common to everybody's experience and on this common ground we can and do meet. The psychologist is a powerful ally for he has discovered much that is common and much that is solely individual in the growth of consciousness in human persons. The Christian will welcome this information even if he has objections to some interpretations put upon it.

"Sexual development," says Schwarz,[2] "follows closely the development of all functions of the personality." As is only too well known, Freud held that all functions of personality were rooted in sexuality. The "libido" or sex urge was the ultimate cause of even the highest activities of the soul. This view did not long satisfy the psychologists. It had always appeared an over-simplification to the

[1] In *Man and Woman*, Longmans, London, 1959.
[2] In *The Psychology of Sex*, Penguin Books, 1949.

metaphysicians. Jung teaches that there is an undifferentiated psychic energy of which sexuality is the first in time of many canalizations. We are not concerned here with appraising different psychological theories but only with such facts as seem firmly established. The most important of these from our point of view is the one stated above by Schwarz. There was a danger in the past that sexuality should be considered as on a par with such appetites as hunger and thirst. Our satisfaction of these is regulated by social custom; we have a reasonable notion of what is excessive in eating and drinking. So too a code of sexual custom should be applicable to every member of the community. Contraventions of this code were looked on either as sins or inevitable weaknesses of the flesh. In other circles they were considered as inevitable vital phenomena; it was absurd to classify them according to a moral theory. On the first view, the glutton, the drunkard and the libertine were sinners, on the second men in whom the life forces happened to be particularly vigorous and insistent. Depth psychology has shown that all three may be, and often are, acting under impulses of which they are not directly conscious. There are drunkards and libertines whose psychological development has been thwarted and who are seeking perfectly legitimate ends by wrong means. A man in childhood may have suffered under a father who was too domineering. The conflict between love and fear of the father may produce a dread of all in authority which can persist throughout life. Such a man may well find he can only face reality when he is in his cups. Another may become homosexual because he was spoiled and cosseted by his mother. Every psychiatrist's case-book is full of cases of this kind.

The importance of our relationships with others, particularly in the early formative years, cannot be exaggerated. As a man is, so does he act. What he is depends very much on what others have made him become. His choices are ultimately his own and free, yet are deeply influenced by forces outside himself. In so far as society as a whole is involved—in the family, the school, the neighbourhood, the parish, etc., we all of us bear some share of responsibility for the personal development of everyone else.

We do not hear enough about this responsibility as far as sex is concerned. The moral law is preached, the commandments taught. When a boy or girl "goes wrong", we are horrified. We tend to think of grace as a preventive medicine which will automatically guarantee against sin. Those who fall must have deliberately chosen to do so with their eyes open. This is certainly true in some cases, but far more often the sin is due to weakness and that weakness may be partly our fault. Those who believe they have a vocation to the religious life are given a long and careful training. It is only recently and in a few places that we are beginning to train our young men and women deliberately and consciously for marriage. Even this is not enough. A new approach is needed. The doctrine is clear, the great dignity of marriage has been taught throughout the Christian ages in spite of violent outbreaks of puritanism. We are coming to realize that the liturgy is not merely a priestly act at which we are to assist as spectators in a suitably devotional but individualistic frame of mind; but it is a community act in which all have their own part to play. So too we must come to see that marriage is not merely a private affair between two persons, but a state for which the Christian community must prepare future brides and bridegrooms and support them in their difficulties once they are married. As long as the sexual climate in our parishes is largely determined by blind custom and lists of taboos, while all the profound significance of sexuality is unknown or unpreached, Christians cannot hope to prevent the prevalent sexual regression.

We go even further. We have referred to Abbé Rambaud's dictum on the natural and good desire which is at the source of sin. We have to discover the good and noble desire which sin is distorting in such abuses as masturbation, contraception and divorce. Far from leading us to condone these, this change of perspective will enable us to help those involved in them to see what the goal for which they are striving by unlawful and frustrating means really and truly is.

A Christian reading a book such as Schwarz's cannot but admire the humanity of the psychologist and yet almost weep at the extremes to which this perfectly honourable sentiment may lead him. We are told, for instance, that a young man cannot expect to have normal and satisfactory sexual relations with his future wife unless he has experimented with other women before marriage. In almost the same breath, Schwarz insists that for women, sexual relationships founded on love have to be thought of as permanent. So, he adds, there must always exist women willing to sacrifice their deepest longings in order to educate young men in the proper use of their sexuality! Yet Schwarz has a point. How are young men, whose psychology is in many respects so different from that of women, to be trained to love their wives fully both physically and spiritually? To the Christian the pre-marital affair will not do for reasons we shall outline in the third section of the book. Nor can we hold that it is sufficient to teach the doctrines we have stated in former chapters. The psychologist will tell us that many of his patients are people who know their Faith, have tried to live up to it, but have met problems arising from temperament or physical maladjustment, and which abstract theology cannot solve.

Masturbation is another of the problems of growth. We

cannot help boys and girls to go through and beyond this crisis, to reach a stage when they become responsible enough to stop the habit without harmful repression, unless and until we know what good urge lies beneath the obsession and how it can be legitimately fulfilled. It is easy enough for the non-Christian to argue that masturbation is an inevitable phenomenon of our growth towards sexual maturity and so should be tolerated as such. Yet this is a lazy way out of the difficulty. It is pure dogmatism to claim that the habit is preparing the child for normal sex relations. The Christian cannot be satisfied with so superficial a view. He wants to know the here and now purpose which lies behind the urge to masturbate. Kinsey here offers him an important fact. It is during the years of adolescence that men are most sexually virile. Yet, as the psychologist insists, underlining what every parent and teacher knows by experience, it is at this period of life that the general character is most unstable and furthest from integration. The notion that society perversely prevents marriage just when young men are physically most capable of intercourse, is not tenable. In human relations, the purpose of sex is not merely to produce children but to beget and rear them in and through a sexuality which is the expression of love. The adolescent is simply not capable of loving in the way marriage requires. It is presumably this fact which prompts psychologists like Schwarz to treat masturbation as an essential stage towards this love. We agree that we must help the adolescent to move in its direction, yet we cannot accept masturbation in itself as anything other than a deviation from the true path. But this we leave to be discussed later in the book.

A Christian is bound to assert that the doctrines of the Fall and the Redemption if rightly understood are of immense psychological importance. If man's passions are good but disordered, if man is redeemed and offered the means to a restoration of the peace which is the tranquillity of order, then to know and act upon these primordial facts will open the way to a full and integrated sexuality. But let the Christian beware! We have already mentioned the superstitious attitude to grace, the idea that it is a magical potion. Grace is all powerful but it can be deflected from the soul by the individual to whom it is offered. The individual lives and acts in societies and groups of various kinds. His reactions to grace are to a great extent conditioned by the ethos of these collectivities. If the adolescent is left to battle alone, unaided, misunderstood, as he struggles with his tempestuous sexuality, resistances to grace are inevitable and overpowering. Nor is it enough to utter pious platitudes about purity and the beauty of true love. He is in no state to combine his passions with love. He almost always knows both of them in their most urgent form and yet sees them as separate and even irreconcilable. It would not be an exaggeration to say that the adolescent male experiences in all their disintegrating ruthlessness, the results of the Fall precisely at the moment when he is drawn to all that is most noble and most pure. In a true sense adolescence is a crucifixion, a tearing apart, a centrifugal crisis, a turmoil of all that is good and evil in man. The great human choices are involved. It is puerile and retrogressive to see masturbation under such circumstances as a mere technical exercise, a prelude to sexual expertise.

It is equally disastrous to look upon it as something too shameful to mention. It is criminal to urge the boy or girl to repress his or her instinctual sex urges. The child must be trained indeed to control instinct. The will must be tempered to cope with the forces of sexuality, but not in isolation from the rest of life. To repress sex, that is, to refuse to face up to it, leads to a hidden conflict that sooner or later will issue in neurosis or behaviour contrary to genuinely human standards. The warfare must be seen in its full context and significance as inevitable during the passage from childhood to manhood. The adolescent is not only a body struggling with its nascent powers, he is also a mind and a spirit at grips with cosmic realities and with the problem of relationship with other people and things. At the same time, he feels alone and hopeless before the urges and stresses of body and mind. He tends to alternate between moods of extreme extraversion and of extreme intraversion. It is difficult to make genuine contact with him. Primitive peoples have initiation rites to deal with this situation. Civilized communities have, rightly or wrongly, abandoned such methods. Yet some form of community action seems called for. It is not the least of Baden-Powell's contributions to modern education that his Scout movement, properly understood and free from false romanticism and naïve nature worship, offers opportunities for a general development of the whole personality. But the sexual problem should not be by-passed or minimized in the process.

Schwarz, in common with other writers, points out that the options presented by sexual growth contain within themselves the essential morality which must govern adult life. We may not agree with him as to all the ethical implications of adolescence but we accept his main contention. The issue is between mammalian instinct and human personality. It is regrettable that Schwarz should condemn whole sections of the population to a permanent fixation in an instinctual life. He plainly does so for he writes:

> The third and by far the largest group patronizing prostitutes is composed of what one may call the "ordinary man in the street". Whereas the adolescent has not yet achieved sexual maturity, and the neurotic is too afraid to attain it, this type of man never does become mature. *The poor substance, the primitive and coarse nature of the*

*personality of these men* bar them from ever reaching the fusion of mind and body which constitutes the perfect adult sexuality. The body seeks its gratification, the mind wants pleasure and the spirit weeps (*op. cit.*, p. 76. Our italics).

This type exists, but the Christian is bound by his faith in God and man to pray and work for its salvation. It may be concern for this "animal" group which has persuaded churchmen in the past to use strong and fear-inspiring methods in dealing with it. In any case, the Christian cannot blithely condemn whole masses of men to this level of existence, as though, by some trick of fate, they are inevitably excluded from the process of love which Solovyev sees as the great evolutionary force of the future. The essential choices come at some time, even if rarely, to every man. However ill-equipped we may be to choose the higher road, each of us is offered the chance to do so at the great moments of crisis. No sexual reform which excludes from its purview the "man in the street" is likely to be of permanent value. If moral theology has something to learn from psychology, psychology has to learn from moral theology that as all things, all men have been redeemed, there can be no lower limit to the scope of the Incarnation. This fact does not make the practical tasks of the moralist any easier, but it does define his full field of reference and of action. Movements such as the Young Christian Workers have accepted the challenge of the masses. These apostles of their own class are surrounded by the "animal" ethos of sexuality and are learning to cope with it. They should be encouraged to seek the truly human urges which lie beneath what appears on the surface as totally inhuman, impersonal, egoistic sexual behaviour.

Here psychology itself, especially in its Jungian form, has much to say. It is true that individual psyches are at every stage of evolution. Some are little more advanced than that of the cave man, others are fixed at a more recent but still clearly bygone level, others again are far ahead of their contemporaries. Yet in them all are certain massive archetypal forces which are always at work in the depths of every human personality. Conscious life may seem to monopolize the energies of a man, but the archetypes are active in his unconscious and issue in the symbolism of his dreams, his longings, his instinctive reactions. However disguised they may be, they are present and constantly placing their immense and healing forces at his disposal.

But they must be recognized and reckoned with. Otherwise, they have a negative and disintegrating effect. In the matter of sex development, the God and the Anima archetypes are of especial importance. A man whose sex life is entirely dominated by the desire for venereal pleasure is thought by many to be behaving like an animal. This is not so, for animals are more or less conditioned by instinctual laws in their sexual activities. The man is under the obsessive influence of a force within him which he does not acknowledge. He is making himself the centre of conscious experience. He is pretending to be God, he is projecting the God archetype in his own unconscious onto his sensations, demanding that other people should be at his service, he is treating his passions and desires as absolute values beyond the scope of question. It may have been an obscure sense of this fundamental blasphemy which gave rise to the ancient institution of temple prostitution. It was perhaps an attempt, however misguided and terrible, to remind men that the gods approve of sex but only in connection with their worship, only when higher values than venereal satisfaction have been acknowledged. The custom, equally abhorrent to the Christian and the humanist, of defloration by a priest is possibly another instance of the same intention. It is found among many non-Christian cultures, and in its distorted way, has this in common with rites such as Jewish circumcision and even Christian baptism—that it shows sex and all that it includes not as having absolute value, but as related to greater and spiritual realities to which it must be subordinated if it is to develop soundly along the line of its own inherent movement.

So far, we have emphasized the masculine pattern of sexual development. We must conclude this chapter with a few notes on sexual differentiation. Anatomically and biologically, there is little difference between the basic structure of the sex organs in male and female. Even the clitoris in the woman is a rudimentary form of the penis and so has an important rôle in intercourse. It would be wrong however to assume that the sexuality of both sexes is also fundamentally the same. Here psychology has said and will have to say a great deal. Briefly, the whole sexual attitude of the woman is determined by her vocation to motherhood. She is the child's first home and on her it will primarily depend during the first and formative years of its extra-uterine life. In Schwarz's words, she is a brain and a womb. Nothing in the man corresponds to the womb. Woman is not only a mammal, she is also, and far more, a place, a person from whose sexuality persons are to be born, nourished and eventually sent into the world to achieve their own maturity. She is caught up physically into the great vital movement of life reproducing itself in countless individuals.

Since this is so, her reaction to sexual stimuli is far less localized than that of the man. Her whole body is involved and, consciously or unconsciously, she expects intercourse to be not only a source of physical satisfaction, of orgasm in the technical sense, but an experience in which her emotional, personal, spiritual nature equally are brought to a unity. For the future mother of persons, the sex acts must be personal too. This is most important. A man may be expert in arousing a woman to the point of physical orgasm and yet fail entirely to achieve this total unity of experience in her. She will be acutely aware that something is wrong. On the other hand, a man may be clumsy and relatively inefficient in the bodily techniques and yet leave her with a sense of contentment, which, imperfect though it is, has called into play the deeper levels of her being. As an ancient marriage rite has it, God has ordained that children shall be born in love. A woman can sense a man's love even if his expression of it in the sex acts is far from adequate. She is then prepared to forgive much. This does not exempt the man from trying to match his physical skill with his spiritual love.

That love demands a full expression, a complete self-giving, much as the basic inspiration of the artist can only be fully realized in the work he is about, if and when the techniques he possesses are so instinctive, so subordinated to the outward movement of the soul towards the material to be changed and given a new and spiritualized form, that he is held back by no obstacles of a physical nature and so can give himself entirely to the work he has undertaken. Only when body and soul are at one in the sexual act of the man can the woman really reach true human orgasm. Only then will she know fully in her flesh the creative urge which is incarnate in her husband and springs both from his personal love for her and from the love of God for all this evolving universe which he has made.

Scientists may discover methods of impregnation that do not require the fertilization of the ova by the spermatozoa. Such a method has already been used in the case of other living creatures. In a sense, the practice of artificial insemination is a step in this direction since it divorces conception from sexual intercourse. It might be inferred from the possibility of chemical or electrical fertilization that intercourse is radically a pleasure mechanism alone, which is only necessary for impregnation because we are not yet aware of any other way of achieving it. In this case, the Catholic view of reproduction as the primary end of marriage may one day be belied by the facts. But is this so? If and when chemical or electrical agents are used t fertilize the woman, will she then willingly abandon herse to what according to this argument is the real primary en of sexual union—the expression of love? We do not think so. Schwarz is surely wrong when he suggests that fertilization without intercourse would raise only sociological problems; it would call into question the relations of man and woman in the sex act. It would involve a divorce between the purely biological phenomena of motherhood and its psychological and spiritual realities. Pleasure would be separated from function. The child would be the product of a scientific mechanism, an artefact. The love of man and woman would be self-contained, ingrowing. There would be a return to a more primitive instinctual life in which love might easily be overpowered by the urges of passion. Under the present dispensation, the possibility of childbirth is a controlling force and, at the same time, opens to the sexual love of the partners the broader prospect of that self-renunciation which is the soul of spiritual love. A genuine, outgoing love between man and his fellow men is, we believe, impossible without the love of man and woman issuing in children, as far at least as the general life of the race is concerned. If this love is confined to the partners and its windows open on to the world forever closed, we face an era of unparalleled selfishness and mental sterility. There is already evidence to suggest that contraception, which is a modified form of this mechanical approach to fertilization, saps the creative forces of any society in which it gains a foothold, and in spheres apparently far removed from sexuality.

It is often argued that the man's part in reproduction,

since it is so infinitesimal from a physical standpoint, proves that fatherhood is a far less powerful force in man than is motherhood in woman. Man in most cultures, though not in all, is the breadwinner, the person who goes out of the home in order to provide for it both economically and morally. It is true that there are primitive peoples among whom the "manly" tasks are performed by women. Nevertheless, the fact of maternity reveals an essential difference between man and woman in every society. Yet if man's generative rôle is reducible to that of the chemical solution of the brave new world of the future, then fatherhood is no more than the fulfilment of a biological function and the "fatherly" tasks are mere products of a cultural code and not rooted in nature.

Some years ago Gabriel Marcel dealt with the question of the vocation to fatherhood in his book *Homo Viator*. The husband, he argues, is far more than a biological agent. He must have "a spontaneous confidence in life, which may be regarded either as a call or an answer to a call. It is through life and through life alone that man can take root in the universe and there develop to his full stature" (*op. cit.*, p. 164). If the father sees the child merely as an extension of himself, he fails in his vocation. He is called by his fatherhood to an act that is a reflection of the great creative will by which the universe was and is created.

Unless a man appreciates this rooting of life in eternity, he will be unable to see his vocation as a father as anything other than a biological and psychological function. If his relations with his children are not based on the sense of an absolute value, he will be little more than a donor of what he wrongly considers his own property. Life is not ours to give; it is a mystery whose origins lie far deeper than the bio-chemical processes through which it manifests itself to our research. If the mother is the place of the child's origin, the father in his own degree is the creative force which peoples that place with life. Should a future technique of fertilization deprive him of his vocation, his creative powers could only be fulfilled—and how inadequately!—in the world of economic competition or, for the few, in that of the plastic arts. And how could a woman continue to love a creature whose primary physical functions were nutrition and non-generative orgastic intercourse? She would see herself as the sole human source of life and of the creative impulse of the race. She would come to consider man as a parasite or a mere purveyor of sensual delight. The immense sociological problems—the control of fertilization, the regulation of intercourse, the possible intrusion of the State into the field of private relations—all imply a degradation of man to the status of an instrument.

It is the transcendent aspect of fatherhood and motherhood which makes it possible for men and women who have not married to realize the creative essence of the married vocation in their own single lives. The tasks of creation are rooted in man's sexual nature but they go far beyond it. The creative work of the father and the mother may be matched in the genuine though "analogical" fatherhood and motherhood of the unmarried who bring an unselfish and outgoing love of others to their work. Our sexual life has been compared to an inverted triangle with its base in the realm of the eternal and its apex in the physical acts of love. When every aspect of our sexuality is permeated by the creative love of persons then the way is open for the sex life of the race to be linked to the "absolute Person who alone can set upon it the unbreakable seal of unity" (G. Marcel, *op. cit.*, p. 170).

# PART III

# SEX AND LIFE

CHAPTER VI

# SEX BEFORE MARRIAGE

Our sexuality allows us to share in the creative and redemptive work of God. The Christian cannot separate the pleasures of sex from its purposes—the begetting of children, the mutual love and integration of husband and wife, the increase of Christ's mystical body, the Church. Our Lord redeems us from within the state of Adam after the Fall. He has not restored to us in this life our full original integrity of soul and body, intellect and will, mind and passions. Redeemed by his suffering and death, we are to be united to him now in our own suffering and death, and in joy and glory in the world to come. Not that this life is nothing but pain and tears. Far from it! The whole sacramental system gives us the substance of everlasting life and eternal joy though in a context of struggle, discipline, agony and finally death.

For many, sexuality is solely or chiefly a means to pleasure considered as an end in itself, and any attempt to bind it to reproduction is thought to be the imposition of a doctrinaire pattern on a biological urge. The birth of children is only one of its many purposes. A moral code which limits it or holds that it is chiefly ordered to one of these only is inhuman.

Faced with such argument, the Christian must beware of two false attitudes. He must not adopt a puritan view of sex, for puritanism narrows the scope of God's purposes and prevents us from seeing life as a whole and redemption as including all man's activities. For the puritan, sex is a scandal. He may even think that intercourse in the human race is the result of original sin. The Catholic knows that this view is heretical. The first principle to grasp is that sex in animals and in men is the means by which God extends his creation throughout time and space. It may be that the intense ánd unique pleasure of sexual intercourse arises from the immense cosmic forces it sets in motion. To experience that pleasure while wilfully defeating the purposes to which it is related is to deny the essential realities of sexual life.

On the other hand, the Christian must not so emphasize the procreative purpose of sex as to forget that to procreate without love is also a perversion. The morality of sex in man depends on what we mean by love. There are only two kinds of love, the love of others and the love of oneself. Both are good, both are necessary. Neither can exist without the other and remain itself. Each must nourish the other. Love of oneself is idolatrous when divorced from love of others. Love of others is mere sentiment and illusion if it does not enrich the self of the lover. Behind others, stands God the infinite Other. We can only truly and fully love ourselves and others in him, who is Love.

For the Christian, sexuality like every other force working in him cannot be separated from the love of God and man. If he is to avoid the false attitudes we have mentioned, he has to see his sexuality as entering into everything he does, for God has made us male and female. The social tasks given to men and women in different cultures may and do vary; the fundamental sexual differentiation remains and marks each sex with an indelible character. He must see his sexuality as an expression of love for others and for God who has given him a sexual nature.

This love will determine when, how, with whom and for what purpose he has sexual relations. Intercourse outside of marriage attacks the divine plan, jeopardizes the work of redemption and prostitutes the woman or the man involved to ends other than those which, as persons made and redeemed by God, they are destined to fulfil.

The Christian cannot accept the view that man is only a superior animal, a sport of evolution, whose sexuality may be used as he thinks fit and for whatever purpose his fancy, whim or hunger for pleasure dictates. To assume this attitude is to deny the facts of revelation and the inherent realities of a rational nature. It reverses the onward course of the evolutionary process which has brought man into the realm of consciousness, ends and choice.

This is not to belittle the facts brought to light by research such as Kinsey's, or the hypotheses of serious psychologists. The Catholic believes in the development of doctrine. The implications of the Incarnation are infinite; Christian doctrine is not a formula relevant only to the times in which it was first promulgated or practicable only in a given cultural, historical setting. Christian dogmas are absolute and unchangeable, but the eternal truths they contain are unfolded and clarified in and through the temporal order. The work of the biologist, the sociologist, the psychologist in so far as it gives us access to positive facts is of value to the process of doctrinal development. This is especially the case in the realm of sex, where doctrine issues in a moral code that concerns everyday life and decisions. We cannot genuinely live and choose if we ignore the realities of our present situation. The twentieth-century Christian has to lead his sexual life in the twentieth century. It is no use for him to pretend that conditions are other than they are or that we know no more about the biological, sociological and psychological facts of sex than did our forefathers. It is equally ridiculous to imagine our ancestors have said nothing of value about sex because they did not know these facts. Our own task is to see and live out the eternal realities in our present historical context, to find the points at which scientific knowledge is illuminated by revelation and those at which scientific knowledge points the way to a deeper understanding of revelation.

It may seem that we are far from the daily round and the common task, from the common man and the common Christian. These do not venture into the high regions of discovery, whether scientific or theological. They face immediate problems or escape from them by leading a life they try to believe is instinctual and natural. Sexual behaviour is largely determined by social custom and the prevalent moral code of the class to which a man belongs. Neither priest nor scientist, we are told, can hope to alter these. But, we ask, who determined this custom and established this code? If they have been imposed in the past by men, there is no reason to suppose that they cannot be changed. The Christian is committed to the fact of grace. By grace the Holy Spirit is present in the soul of the redeemed. The sacraments of the Church are not mere rituals or magic incantations, they confer power, they make it possible for man to reach his full stature as sharer in the creation and redemption. Therefore sexual problems raise one fundamental question—what are the obstacles to grace which make difficult the full sex life as God intends it to be, and how are they to be overcome? In other words, what must the twentieth-century Christian do so that grace may guide and direct him in his sexual life under the conditions of the present time?

For the Catholic, grace is inseparable from the Church; it is an individual gift and a social force. It enables him to serve his fellow Christians, it links and joins him with

Christ the Head of the mystical body and so with all the members of that body. He cannot look upon his own or others' sex lives as purely individual. He cannot believe he is responsible for his own sex conduct alone. This is too often forgotten and much of the sexual chaos of today is the result of selfish individualism on the part of Christians.

In this final section, we shall attempt to outline some of the difficulties the Christian meets in his sex life and examine some of the obstacles on which he stumbles and often falls. We shall try to suggest how these difficulties are to be overcome and the obstacles circumvented. Above all, we shall ask how the Christian's love for God and his fellow men help him towards an integrated sexuality, fully human and fully Christian. This is a formidable undertaking and we do not pretend to have provided more than a sketch plan of an enormous field of experience and endeavour. Further, there is the danger that besets all writing on sex—readers are likely to expect that their own individual problems will be automatically solved for them. General principles are easy enough to state, but the great variation in individual reactions to circumstance and situation makes it impossible to issue a guidebook to sexual conduct.

We can only hope to show the Christian reader what sexuality is fundamentally, what options it presents, and then we must leave him to work out his own pattern for himself. Or better still, we may hope to have done a little towards establishing a truly Christian "climate" of sexuality, so that those who are growing to adult status may be helped as they face the challenge of our century, in which they have to live and to witness to God, Creator and Redeemer. We must insist again that to make life obedient to love is a major project. In all fields we are constantly failing in this attempt, not least in that of sex. But to fail is not to despair. In our sex life, as in every other realm of experience and action, we must go on, and go on going on, in our God–given vocation of restoring all things in Christ, the king of love.

Our first problem is in a sense the most important. How are we to give our children sex education? It seems odd that after all these centuries we should still be asking it. Little is known as to whether or how our ancestors provided their children with any formal instruction in sex matters. It is usually assumed that they did nothing about it. Most of the readers of this book will have learned of sex from other children while at school. Yet the popes of recent years have insisted that it is the duty of parents to prepare their children for their sex lives.

We believe the question is wrongly framed. It implies to most people nothing but the problem of how to tell children the facts of intercourse. This, it is assumed, is the basis of sex education, and it is most difficult to communicate. If it is only a matter of biological information, the parents' embarrassment is understandable. Sex matters are so cluttered up with taboos and false shame that embarrassment is inevitable. Apart from the delicate sexual relationship between parents and children which already sets up an obstacle to instruction, the telling of the bald physical facts of intercourse to the child only gives him a small part of the whole story. Intercourse is the expression of an adult love and the child cannot grasp how or why this is so, for he has had no experience of the love which seeks this form of expression. Yet, if we wait until he has, he may have already taken a false path and our task will then be partly remedial and so far more difficult.

The boy and girl on the threshold of puberty are no longer the self-centred beings they were during infancy. They have begun to love and to realize that love is a giving as well as a receiving. They have learned that it demands sacrifice and the discipline of wishes and desires. It is on this knowledge that a sound sexual education can and must be based. We have to build on the child's experience of love for others and to encourage him to make sacrifices and so to practise a fruitful, life-giving asceticism. Soon, the great sexual urge will become a physical reality for him. Unless he is able to relate it to unselfish love, he will regress sexually to infantile self-seeking and risk remaining fixed in this initial stage of his evolution.

Everything will depend on his relations with his parents. If there is mutual love and confidence between them, if he senses that he himself is caught up in the love which they have for each other, if he knows his parents are ready and willing to answer his questions, to understand the problems which are so terrifying to him and so insignificant to the adult, then he will ask for the information which he needs at the time when he feels he wants it.

It cannot be too strongly emphasized that a man's sexuality and sexual behaviour are the expression of the kind of love that directs his life. A spoiled child on the one hand and one who is dominated by his parents on the other, are both driven in upon self-love. To tell them the facts of intercourse will only provide them with a technique by means of which they can find in their own bodies that sense of delight and satisfaction their parents deny them in other spheres of life. Sex education has to be seen in the context of the whole developing personality and as part of that process of growth. Unless the child is constantly encouraged by precept and example to love, we cannot do much to help him face the upsurge of passion when it comes.

A truly Christian spirituality of marriage and parenthood includes a genuine appreciation of the grace given when the sacrament of matrimony is received. This grace gives husband and wife the power and the duty to love each other and their children unselfishly and with full mutual confidence and trust. They have always to fight the impulse to self-centred love, the greatest obstacle to their own union and to the healthy growth of their children. If they are ashamed of their own sexuality, or if, on the contrary, they treat it merely or chiefly as a pleasure mechanism, they are the last persons to train their children to love. The responsibility of parents is immense. The criminally infantile attitude to sex which is characteristic of our society makes their task still more difficult. As we have already written, a new climate of sexuality is essential in the home and in the street. To imagine that a course of biology lessons will be sufficient equipment for a child on the threshold of the puberty crisis is to be singularly naïve.

If, however, the personal relationships between parent and child are sound, the biological facts can be communicated in much the same way as other information. All healthy children want to know how things work. They are also incurable metaphysicians, always wanting to discover causes. Their own origins are just another problem for which they ask an explanation. We have to see that they are told the whole truth, that sexuality is revealed to them in its full context of creation and redemption, of body and soul. We must not fob them off with old wives' tales or throw the physical facts at them to make what they can of them. This integrated sexual instruction cannot be given all at once, although it is amazing how satisfied a child may be with only one explanation provided it is offered simply and objectively and includes all the levels of meaning which human sexuality possesses.

Parents are probably more worried by the masturbation bogey than by anything else in this matter of sex education. Can children be prevented from masturbating by being warned beforehand? Where there is complete trust between parents and children, this is a reasonable hope. Parents must remember, however, that if their hopes are disappointed, if the child does fall into the habit in spite of their warning, they must not attempt to cure him by threats, bullying, contempt and the like. We owe doctors and sexologists a debt of gratitude for revealing the almost universal extent of the masturbation habit among boys. Facts such as those collected by Kinsey should make it clear to every parent that his child is not a monster. How many children have been tortured by the belief that they alone had acquired this habit and so were a disgrace to their families!

Yet the Christian cannot accept the irresponsible attitude of those who say that the child should not be interfered with at all, since the habit will pass and he will be none the worse for it. Personality is attained by constant effort and struggle. We have to help the young to achieve true, vital chastity in spite of masturbation. To tell them it is of no importance whether they masturbate or not will leave them with the idea that sexuality is a force beyond human control. This may lead them to accept and to follow every kind of sex urge in later life with no thought of the suffering or harm they may cause to others.

How each individual is to be helped to master the urge without unhealthy repression, false thinking and a negative sense of guilt, depends largely on the circumstances in each case. No general rule can be laid down. Parents, doctors, confessors, teachers, all need to study the problem much more and together. A fuller analysis of the multiple phenomena of puberty and adolescence would reveal the profound play of forces striving to come up into consciousness at this period of life. Masturbation would be seen as offering a challenge to the growing child. His later development as a person will depend to a great extent not so much on *whether* he masters it, important though this is, as on *how* he masters it. It is better for him to fail again and again and yet to know what this failure means in relation to his whole personality, rather than to succeed by stern repression that will leave the vital metaphysical and spiritual problems of which masturbation is the outward sign unresolved and working like a poison in the unconscious mind.

It is fatally easy for parents, teachers and even confessors to assume that because by threats and an insistence on the negative aspect of sin they have driven the child to abandon the habit, a great victory had thereby been won for chastity. Nothing could be further from the truth. Mere outward conformity with no trace of inward conviction is contrary to everything the Christian faith stands for. Although Christ has not restored to us our original gift of integrity, he has provided the means of grace to help us to recover more and more of that happy state as our life develops. Such an achievement demands struggle, but it is essentially *not* a struggle against life but towards an ever increasing love, it is not a negative repression of urges which are only evil in so far as they tend to seek their own ends apart from the full individual and social nature of the human person as a potential unity of experience and existence. It is precisely here that the Christian doctrine of marriage is so relevant.

Our Lord not only restored marriage to its original status and indeed gave it a far nobler one, he also—and by the same token—revealed the whole direction of personal integration in the sexual life. Sex is made whole by the love of one man for one woman. In that love it is gathered together and orientated in a single act by means of which all the dispersive and disintegrating forces of passion are checked, reassembled and focused on to one endeavour, and made to enter the realm of an abiding love. From centrifugal, the sex urges become centripetal. The root of sex education at every period of life is therefore the conquest of a genuine love both for oneself and for others.

Before we consider the fact and implications of hetero-sexual attraction, one difficulty must be faced. Kinsey's researches make it obvious that homosexuality is far more prevalent than is generally thought. He claims that it is unscientific to look on this type of sexual behaviour as an aberration or as inevitably perverse. It is untrue, he main-tains, to believe that there is strictly speaking any such person as a homosexual man or woman. There are homo-sexual habits, but these are no more abnormal than mas-turbation or extra-marital intercourse. To the Christian, this information is good news since it enables us to include the problem of homosexual conduct in the general scope of a Christian ethic. We are not obliged to consider those who indulge in it as doomed by some freak of nature to behaviour that goes counter to the whole purpose of sex for the individual and the race.

Many psychologists believe that homosexual behaviour results from a distorted emotional development. Here, as with masturbation, much can be done to persuade the child to abandon it if his difficulties are understood and he realizes that we understand and sympathize with him at this critical time. However, the main trouble, as we know all too well, is that the child rarely confides in his elders. His sexual habits remain a secret. It is generally assumed that this is inevitable since the child is now beginning to feel the growing strength of his own personality and is moving towards complete independence. This is doubtless true, but it does not follow that the puberty and adolescent sexual stages have to be lived through in total isolation from adults. As long as sex is considered as taboo, this false belief will continue to deprive young people of the help they need. How frank and healthy communication between adolescents and adults is to be established is one of the major problems of human relations in our culture and time. Far too little serious thought is given to it. Adults tend to shift the responsibility on to one another. It is the parent's business, says the teacher, the teacher's, says the parent, or the priest's or the doctor's, the scoutmaster's or the youth leader's. It is everybody's business and it is high time this were realized. We hope that in pre-marital training courses, some attempt is being made to deal with the problem.

Homosexual behaviour is more common than we suppose, yet it is confined to a minority. For most young persons the other sex alone attracts. Here one of the most burning questions of the day confronts the Christian. Kinsey shows that the incidence of sexual intercourse before marriage is on the increase. Moreover, the habit of petting is becoming commoner, particularly in the more educated sections of the population in the U.S.A., where it is practised as a substitute for intercourse. The Christian is criticized by many when he questions the morality of petting in its more advanced forms and altogether condemns pre-marital coitus. The arguments used to justify both are powerful and cannot be met by mere dogmatic proclamation. The advocates of what the Christian is bound to call sexual laxity claim that petting to a point just short of coitus and pre-marital intercourse itself are necessary stages on the way to marriage. The technique of love-making, it is argued, is of great importance for the happy relations of man and wife in their future union, and it is unrealistic to expect young men and women to acquire this technique only after their wedding. The Christian may not deny the importance of love-making in all its aspects, physical and spiritual. But his opponents are equally bound to avoid over-emphasizing the rôle of the body in sexual relationships at the expense of the more fundamental and lasting personal issues involved. Neither is it legitimate to point to primitive customs and to insist that the sexual impulses in the adolescent period demand an uncontrolled and full outlet because they are at maximum intensity and promiscuous in character. Later, we are told, young people will adjust themselves adequately to the requirements of the married life. We cannot accept this argument for our culture is not primitive and coital prowess is no justification for irrational behaviour. The greatest achievement of western society is its concern for the individual and personal values, and in any case there is not sufficient evidence to prove that marriages are happier if one or both partners have given more or less unchecked rein to their sexual desires before marriage.

The Christian attitude to petting and pre-marital intercourse is based on the full facts of human sexuality as redeemed by Christ. If young people are trained in positive chastity, if they are taught to realize that their sexuality reaches its climax in the handing on of life by and through their love for their married partner, they have at least a directive norm in their pre-marital relationships with those of the opposite sex.

When a man enters the territory of another personality both physically and spiritually as he does in sexual intercourse if it is in any sense human, then he steps beyond the limits of his own ego into the infinite realm of the Other. One woman is not only enough to lead him to, keep him in and help him to journey further into this realm, she is also the only, the strait, the narrow gate leading to this infinite life, this ever-expanding consciousness. Promiscuity, however charged with erotic emotion, reverses this process. The multiplicity of creatures is an image, a refraction of the simplicity of the absolute God, who alone holds all creation in his contemplation of himself and so can see their unity in diversity. Creatures cannot in this life enjoy such perfect contemplation over the whole range of created being. To seek a knowledge of the depths of human personality in its full incarnate nature by means of promiscuity is therefore a prime example of that desire to be as gods which caused the Fall of Adam. Unity of experience in the sexual sphere can only be found in fidelity to one person. Promiscuity drives us back to the disintegrated and disintegrating succession of ephemeral sensations and emotions, to the world of the *schlechte Unendlichkeit*, the evil infinity. Fidelity alone leads us to the eternal.

In so far as the techniques of sexual stimulation and the achievement of the female orgasm are important elements in married life, as they most certainly are, the young couple should be told about them. If they have accepted the duty of reverence towards the persons of others they will not wish to use bodies and personalities as mere material for experiment. Engaged couples need to be told that when they are married they will have to learn the art of love-making in all its aspects together and from one another. It is special pleading to claim that it should be learned outside of marriage, while all the other adjustments can only be brought about by the day to day experiences of married life. Neither these nor love-making are likely to come easily.

We have already pointed out that the "mores" in respect of the degree of intimacy in the marriage act differ in different sections of society. Kinsey's statistics place this fact beyond question. Many couples, whatever their views on petting and pre-marital intercourse, will refuse to prac-tise certain techniques of stimulation because the prevalent belief in their class of society holds them to be perversions. On the other hand priests, doctors, friends who are asked for advice, may themselves come from social classes where it is still considered that anything more than a direct and speedy coitus is undesirable, and so have no sympathy with those who have been taught the opposite. There is need here for great delicacy and careful handling of a very real problem. Catholic moral theologians are agreed that any gestures inspired by love and directed to procreation are legitimate in marriage. Yet the Pauline principle remains relevant—a thing may be lawful but inexpedient. In so far as objections to intimacies arise from false notions of sexual morality, they must be countered by sound doctrine. At the same time, it is imprudent to urge young people indiscriminately and without preparation towards behaviour which they have been brought up to consider as perverse and which therefore they might practise with wrong intentions.

It is often said that the young Christian engaged couple should look upon the engagement period as a kind of noviciate for the married state. Put thus baldly, the statement is unconvincing, even ludicrous. Yet, when examined more closely and realistically, it is seen to be profoundly true. The religious novice is trained in the spiritual and physical patterns of conduct and attitude necessary for his life in the order or institute of which he or she hopes to become a permanent member. Marriage is an institution older than any religious order and has both spiritual and physical requirements. Fiancés should know what these are and be prepared for the life they involve.

There is one obvious distinction between the religious noviciate and that of the engaged couple. The religious novice is separated from the everyday world and is under the care of an experienced religious who can help him or her to face the inevitable trials and difficulties met in the common life of the institute. The engaged couple normally see one another only in the evenings, they spend most of the day at their trade or profession, and they have no novice master or mistress. All the more reason, therefore, why the engagement period should be taken seriously and not as a sort of inhibited rehearsal for the honeymoon. It is to be regretted that the former Catholic practice of solemn betrothal before a priest has largely lapsed. Clearly the Church believes that there are special graces and blessings for those who are about to marry. It is still more regrettable that families, parishes and Catholic societies do little or nothing to help the engaged. They are obviously in need of advice of all kinds, economic, medical, psychological and spiritual. They are generally left to muddle through as best they can.

We are not suggesting a prying interference in the affairs of other people. It is a matter of the whole approach of our society, religious and lay, towards marriage and sex and what they involve in the way of personal and social values. Realistic appreciation of truth eventually becomes incarnate in concrete institutions and bodies of custom. The peculiar and ever-changing pattern of modern life demands a conscious effort to bring the Christian doctrine of marriage and sexual morality into the light of day. We need a positive, vital approach based on sound theology, sound psychology, sound sociology, sound physiology and above all on a heightened sense of our responsibility for the future happiness and personal development of those about to be married. In such a frank and healthy atmosphere, excessive petting and pre-marital intercourse will cease to be regarded as delectable though forbidden fruits. They will be seen for what they are—inadequate, make-shift, irresponsible solutions to genuine problems.

Here, as throughout this section, we must remember that the sacraments are not merely individual gifts. We do not receive them solely for our own personal benefit. Each of them has an immense social significance and imposes on us obligations towards other people and gives us the grace to fulfil them. In examining our consciences we ask ourselves whether we have committed any sexual sin. How often do we inquire whether we have omitted to do all in our power to make sexual life easier for others? The cult of individualism and a spirituality of self-regarding anxiety has its most sinister repercussions in the sexual realm. We are only too prone to be pharisees and to pride ourselves on being more pure than "this publican", this boy who is struggling to make love, not lust, his guide, this woman who has fallen into adultery. Nor need we smugly reply that we are entitled to cast a stone since we are without sin. Our very failure to produce a society (even in our own families and parishes) where sex can reach its full and noble redeemed stature, proclaims that we are not.

# CHAPTER VII

# SEX IN MARRIAGE

It has become increasingly clear that those not in union with us in faith may admire and even accept most of the articles of our creed, but will refuse to follow us in our doctrine and ethic of marriage. Many who have come all the way with us up to this point in the argument will now turn sadly away. Contraception, divorce, even perhaps extra-marital intercourse, will seem to them inevitable given the conditions of human life. Not that they will approve of them as general principles; rather will they maintain that there are times and occasions when they cannot be avoided in particular and hard cases. Hence they have to be occasionally tolerated if not openly preached.

It is useless for the Catholic to meet this challenge with legal formulas. These enshrine a whole philosophy and theology of human life. They are in no sense a substitute for them. Unless we face the genuine difficulties which cause our non-Catholic friends to allow exceptions to the normal law, unless we can show them that our solutions are alone fully human, we should do better to say nothing.

Since the Catholic morality of sexual behaviour is based on the fact that sexual activity is to be directed to procreation through love, it follows that there is no fundamental difference between our sexual code in marriage and out of it. The married have no more right than the unmarried to use their sexual powers for self-seeking or purposes wilfully opposed to procreation. If we abandon this principle, particularly if we practise any form of contraception, we are attempting to give to a spiritual and biological force an end which it does not of itself possess. Human ingenuity is made to replace a divine law. An act which should be entirely governed by love becomes no more than an act of shared pleasure. The status of sex is reduced to that of a private habit which we regulate according to our own desires and circumstances. We are in a world of triviality and whim. Our human stature is debased and cheapened. The relationship between man and woman is taken out of the great cosmic stream of love and life and becomes an affair of convenience and calculation. The contraceptive couple refuses the mutual self-giving, the conscious acceptance of the whole dimension of human love. Sexual intercourse is a backwater of petty bargaining and puerile caution.

But, it will be objected, there are insuperable obstacles of every kind in the way of this full abandonment to the claims of love. Contraception may be regrettable but it is inevitable. We are in no situation to attempt the impossible. The Catholic view sets an ideal before us which is in fact unattainable. And is it really a human ideal? Is it not reasonable that men and women should refuse to procreate like animals? Should they not plan their families rationally and responsibly in the best interests of all concerned? Is not this just what a genuine love demands? Does not the Catholic Church preach the abandonment of all prudence and an indulgence in intercourse with no regard to the needs of wife and children? Is not contraception a reasonable and realistic solution to the problem of reconciling instinctual drives with rational foresight?

No one in his senses can deny that it is difficult for many people to have large families under the unfavourable conditions of modern times in the English-speaking world. Nor can we expect heroic virtue save in the few. In any case, is it heroic to have a large family when we know that it is next to impossible to give each child its fair share?

There is a misunderstanding here. The Catholic Church does not recommend the founding of a large family regardless of any considerations other than the biological urge, nor does she teach that faith and confidence in God's providence excludes all prudence and forethought. On the contrary, it is as un-Christian to give way to sexual impulses without love for wife and children as to take refuge in the selfish unproductive contraceptive marriage. What is taught is that, all allowances being made for the claims of love, the large family of itself offers the best environment for a healthy growth from infancy to maturity, and not least because it is founded on a spirit of generosity and self-sacrifice in the parents. It does not follow, however, that a large family is a sign that contraception has been avoided. The spacing of births, even if they are numerous, may have been brought about by contraceptive methods. Spacing is almost always necessary, but must be achieved in accordance with two principles—it must be for the greater good in every way of *all* concerned, and must be the result of methods that are ethically sound.

Fr Archambault has pointed out that the researches of Pearl of the U.S.A. in 1939 show that on an average 301 acts of intercourse are necessary for one live birth. This figure contradicts the assumption of the advocates of contraception. Their literature appears to take it for granted that without contraception the married couple cannot avoid an annual pregnancy. Pearl's statistics give the average number of children in the non-contraceptive family as seven. The expectation is therefore in the range of one childbirth every two years, which gives an average of three coitus per week. If this rate is reduced by half, the average is likely to fall to one birth every four years. As Archambault remarks, this is to ask for less restraint than that required by the Ogino or "rhythm" method.[1]

This is illuminating yet the fact remains that there is such enormous variation in the coitus rate of the human male that to ask for even this apparently moderate degree of asceticism is to demand of some heroic virtue. There are cases of Catholic couples caught between two fires— if they continue to have children, it will be at the price of the health of the wife while, if they do not, there is the risk of exposing the husband to strong temptations.

The question of the force and frequency of sexual urges needs thorough investigation. It is believed that all sorts of extraneous factors contribute to the degree of erotic response in the human male. Environment, the strain, rush and sheer noise of the modern city may have considerable influence. The general erotic character of advertisement, the frustration resulting from much of the monotonous work men have to do—all these and other influences may be partly responsible for impulses which it is all but impossible to control. At the same time, endocrine factors play a large part, and in this field there is much still to be discovered, which might open the way to remedial treatment.

Meanwhile men and women have to live and meet their problems day by day. How can they be helped to subordinate their sexuality to love? How can they be saved from the agonizing experience of finding that the physical union which is the expression of their love runs counter to that love in its broader aspects and implications? The contraceptive methods may appear to give a simple and effective solution but, in fact, they beg the whole question. They are a concrete denial in the flesh of the nature and scope,

[1] In *Limitation des Naissances et conscience Chrétienne*, Éditions Familiales de France, Paris, 1950, p. 57.

the character and status of human love. They give free rein to the instincts and dehumanize them. They virtually affirm that man is not obliged in his sex life to choose his course of action in accordance with the laws of his psycho-somatic and spiritual nature. To plan births by artificial means, to deprive intercourse of its full biological function, is to separate sexual pleasure from the most obvious and fundamental purpose of sexual union.

Many of those who practise contraception are aware of this. It is not uncommon to find that the use of chemical methods and of contraceptive apparatus is eventually abandoned in favour of coitus interruptus on the grounds that there is something distasteful and unworthy of human intercourse in the former. With the improvements in the conditions of life brought about by modern social legislation and progress, every form of artificial birth prevention is becoming a matter of custom, at least in England. To produce a large family is looked upon as a sign of stupidity or weakness and is fast becoming taboo. It is not done. What the consequences of such an anti-human attitude are likely to be is a matter needing thorough and scientific investigation. A human ecology would have to take into account the implications of this denial of a root principle of biological law.

We do not deny that there are real problems, individual and social, which prompt men and women to adopt contraceptive techniques, even if they feel these are undesirable in themselves. There is always need for some kind of control over sexual activity and its results. The argument against contraception is that it controls the results without controlling the activity. As Pearl's statistics show, there is a natural way of spacing births. It requires what to most men is a moderate exercise of restraint. For those who still feel such a method is uncertain, there is the Safe Period. This is allowed by Catholic moral theology. As our attitude in this matter is often misunderstood and criticized as essentially contraceptive, the position must be briefly stated.

The morality of any action depends upon intention and on the nature of the act itself. An immoral act may be performed with a good intention. It is none the less immoral. A moral act may be performed with a bad intention and so itself becomes subjectively immoral. A man may kill an incurable invalid in order to put him out of his suffering. This is murder even if we call it "mercy killing". We may use the Safe Period in order to avoid the responsibilities of parenthood. The use of the Safe Period then becomes immoral and the sexual acts as "unnatural" in the broadest sense as any contraceptive technique, although the coitus itself is legitimate. The Catholic couple have no right to practise safe period intercourse for purely selfish reasons. Nor are they entitled to avoid births because they lack the spirit of generosity. There are valid reasons based on a genuine concern for the welfare of the partner and of the children which justify care in the spacing of pregnancies. As Pius XII pointed out, there are even cases where Safe Period intercourse is indicated during the whole time of the woman's fertility. The essential rule is that spacing must be undertaken for humane and human reasons; it must be prompted by genuine, unselfish love on the part of both partners.

The Ogino method cannot be properly called contraceptive. The fact that in the majority of cases there is a definable period in the menstrual cycle which is infertile, makes it possible for the marriage act to take place without the immediate prospect of a possible pregnancy. As the Catholic Church teaches that "mutual aid" is one of the ends of marriage, intercourse at this time serves that end, although it is unable to fulfil the primary biological purpose of generation. Our case against contraception is that it *does not* fulfil the secondary aim, since it sets up an *artificial* barrier, physical and psychological, between the partners at the very moment when they should be most united—and this is true even of coitus interruptus, if only at the psychological level. We would agree that if a Catholic couple constantly uses the Ogino method for the wrong reasons, if the partners make "mutual aid" of set purpose the only end of their marriage, then they are introducing another sort of bar to perfect union. The only exception is the case of those who through no fault of their own are childless. For them the secondary end is the only one available as far as intercourse is concerned.

There is a real need, as Pius XII pointed out, for a thorough investigation of the Ogino method, its limitations, its efficacy, its physical and psychological effects. There can be no doubt that there must be and always has been some kind of social and corporate control over the birth rate. Our medieval ancestors achieved this by a severe restriction of the marriage rate. Certain members of the family were prevented from marrying. The power of the father in a society based on land tenure was so great that he was able to decide which of his children should marry and which should not, and then impose his will on them all. The great religious orders must have housed many who originally came to them because of such a parental decision. The number of births was roughly determined by the social structure of the peasant state, and the method of restriction, involving stresses, frustration and suffering, was the control of the marriage rate. It is important for Catholics to realize this. Some are too prone to look back on a non-existent, imaginary past where they believe no sexual problems existed and no effort was made to control the number of births. This leads them to advocate a trust in Providence which is little more than "tempting" God.

The rise of modern industrial society and the proletariat

has introduced the custom of "freedom of marriage". In most cases, the parents have scarcely any say in the matter. And so, the modern personal and social problems arise—sexual urges, inadequate housing, the welfare of the children—and make it possible for the advocates of artificial birth prevention to gain a ready hearing. The Catholic must recognize the existence and the urgency of these problems. He must not preach imprudence in the name of an abandonment to Divine Providence which is really nothing of the kind, but rather a refusal to accept the responsibilities of the human state. We must not fob our people off with ready made answers which, valid enough as general principles, have to be applied to concrete situations very different from those of the Middle Ages or even of Victorian times.

As we see it, the Catholics of England and the U.S.A. have to face a major task. They must always see sexuality and generation as inseparable from love. While we cannot refuse to be generous in the handing on of the gift of life, we must realize that this generosity does not include a thoughtless and irresponsible abandonment to a biological urge. Love does not work in that way. We shall admit that some kind of control over the birth rate is a duty of mankind, but we shall fight with all our might against methods which are dehumanizing and immoral. We have to preach and practise a joyful, positive, manly asceticism in *all* our life. Without it love, as we see it to be, cannot direct our sexual activities. In a word, we have to challenge the family planners on their own ground and show them that, in so far as they advocate contraceptive techniques, they are reducing the whole complex question of personal relationships between husband and wife to a problem of mechanics. Control when we are concerned with vital and spiritual realities like love, human sexual intercourse, childbirth, is not to be compared with the control of a mechanical structure. The human body is not a machine inhabited by an engineer called the soul. It is the place of incarnation, the organ which gives flesh and blood to the deeper purposes, intentions and decisions of the soul. Human love in its sexual form is incarnate in the biological structure of the bodily organism. Control in this sphere is analogous to the exercise of authority, and the whole aim of authority, as its Latin derivation suggests, is to increase, to favour the full and harmonious growth of those over whom it has to be exercised.

The Ogino method, when used with the right intention, does not attack the heart of the relationship between husband and wife as do the contraceptive techniques. It remains within the terms of reference of the biological law. It does not replace a vital and spiritual reality by a technical dodge.

At the same time, we must try to remedy those faults in the social structures which lead to a restriction of births beyond what should be normal in a healthy and vigorous community. To take only one instance, it is no use attacking contraception and then stand calmly by while young married couples are herded into three-roomed flats!

If Catholics in the English-speaking world face and shoulder their responsibilities in this great matter, the effect upon the general population might well be far-reaching. Many are uneasy about contraception but cannot see any workable alternative. It is for us to prove that the need for limitation may not be so urgent as they imagine—and this we can only do by objective research and by working for a social order which will place the sexual problems in their right context, in the sphere of love and relationship. And in cases of ill-health, personal sexual difficulties, genuine economic stresses and family needs, which a more just and rational order of society would still fail to alleviate, we must be able to offer the real and complete facts of the Safe Period. This calls for painstaking and accurate research into the Ogino method on the part of Catholic scientists and sexologists.

The divorce figures for the English-speaking world in general prove that a considerable number of marriages break down. In this book we are concerned primarily with sexuality as such rather than with the specific difficulties of family relationships. Yet it is a fact that sexual incompatibility is responsible, if not for the majority of broken marriages, at least for a high proportion of them. In most cases, it is a contributory factor. Marriage guidance counsellors find that women who experience full sexual satisfaction in intercourse with their husbands rarely leave them, while those who have deserted their husbands for lack of true orgasm and have found the latter in the company of another man, will never agree to return.

Sexual frustration may be experienced, though in different ways, by either of the partners. A man may be highly sexed and his wife far less so. This is a situation frequent enough to call for much sympathy and understanding on the part of wives. On the other hand, the so-called "frigidity" of many women may be and often is due to the lack of skill on the part of the man, whose impatience, or lack of knowledge or social inhibitions prevent him from stimulating his wife to the point of orgasm. But she too may be the victim of her upbringing or temperament and so be unwilling to accept the perfectly legitimate attentions of her husband which she wrongly considers improper. In a book like this, it is not possible to go into detail. We can only note that—with the proviso already made regarding class "mores" in this respect—it is essential that engaged and married couples should be told of the full requirements of the human act of intercourse and given, in the case of the man, some help in training the body to respond to love rather than to external stimuli.

Kinsey has shown that the huge spate of pornographic literature and illustration which exists not only in its own right but in more or less modified forms all around us in advertisements, entertainment, etc., is addressed solely to the male population. Women—except in the relatively rare cases of homosexuals—are not influenced by this type of stimulus. As Bergson remarked, western society is steeped in eroticism, and encourages a prurient, adolescent attitude to one of the most responsible and adult activities of the human race. It may seem unrealistic to insist that Catholics must do something about this. If we attempt to turn back the tide of puerile irresponsibility, if we seek to oppose this mass wave of exploitation of a basic urge for commercial gain, we are accused ourselves of refusing to be adult! It is unfortunately true that some of our efforts in this direction have been none too happy. It is useless to draw up codes of decency that only deal with superficial mani-festations and leave the profoundly impure and inhuman forces at work in our society untouched and even un-recognized. Nor is it prudent to attack genuine efforts in literature and art to deal frankly with the facts of the sexual situation. We must not set out to "de-sex" society —a blasphemous and impossible project—but rather strive to humanize the western approach to sex. As things stand, much of the humanist and Christian activity in this field is bogged down in sentimentality or a residual puritanism that provides remedies as bad as the disease.

Whatever the cause of the increase in the divorce rate, the fact remains that, for the Catholic, divorce in the sense of a separation conferring the right to remarry is not merely unlawful but impossible. The Catholic Church upholds the right of the married to undertake an obligation beyond the jurisdiction of both civil and ecclesiastical courts. Unless a man and woman enter into marriage with a final and irrevocable oath of lifelong fidelity, the union is invalid from the start. Nor is the failure of one party to keep the vow sufficient reason for absolving the other from his or her obligation. The promise engages the whole personality before God and he alone can abrogate it.

This seems a stern doctrine in view of the numerous hard cases which lead our contemporaries to approve the divorce legislation of the modern state. Nor are they mollified when we explain that divorce in the sense of separation "from bed and board" is permitted by the Church for a grave reason, although without the right of remarriage during the lifetime of either partner. This, they argue, is to condemn the innocent to what may, in the event, prove to be permanent abstinence or irregular sexual intercourse. It also prevents the separated parties from achieving legally by a new marriage the primary end of the institution —the birth of children.

The Church has no choice. She dare not refuse to men and women the power to make a permanent pledge, nor claim the right to annul a vow which is registered in the realm of the eternal. She insists that although the love of man and wife is normally expressed in sexual union, the latter is subservient to the former, which can remain when sexual union for whatever reason becomes impossible. Christ has wedded the human race; marriage is the divinely appointed sign of that divine-human union. For those who cannot continue to live together, the only way is that of renunciation, the way of Christ crucified, who is indissolubly linked to our race in spite of the refusal of the majority of men to acknowledge him as their Redeemer and their Head.

The grace of our Lord enables the innocent victims of discord and infidelity to keep their vow and their love. It is equally true that the Christian community receives the

grace and the obligation to help men and women called
to this bitter way of renunciation and suffering. We are
commanded to "bear one another's burdens". One of the
most terrible scandals is our failure to do this, especially
in the case of broken marriages. We forsake our Lord's
suffering members and flee.

Freud's theory of the sublimation of sexual urges in
other types of activity may or may not be true. The view
of those who hold that sexual abstinence means the death
of all genuine sexuality may be right, at least where such
abstinence is forced upon an unwilling victim and is not
the act of perfect self-surrender to love which characterizes
the vow of chastity when freely taken. Nonetheless, the
fact that the vocation of fatherhood and motherhood can
be genuinely fulfilled by adoption where couples are childless, shows that the long experience of the race recognizes
that the purpose of sex can be achieved to some degree
apart from the fruitful biological union. The Christian
community should discover ways and means of helping
those whose marriages have broken down to find in other
spheres of life the substance of the love whose physical
expression is no longer possible in the married state.

The mention of adoption brings us to the sad case of
those who desire children but have not had them. Our
modern society, with its admirable concern for those who
are suffering, but with its desperate lack of understanding
of the full estate of fallen and redeemed mankind, has
sought and found a technique partially to meet this problem—artificial insemination. Here again, the position of
the Catholic Church is misunderstood and misinterpreted.
There is no logical consistency, it is urged, in her argument.
On the one hand she condemns those who practise contraception in order to avoid childbirth, while at the same time
she forbids those who want children to use a medical
technique which will achieve what normal relations have

failed to do. The contradiction is only apparent. Both condemnations have the same basis. The Church believes in the infinite value of every human person. She is committed to the realistic view of the human state, to the fact that, though redeemed, we are not restored in this life to our original integrity. She upholds the rights of human love in the sphere of sex, and insists that all sexual activity must be dominated by that love and in the context of the biological forces in which it is situated. She encourages the doctor to do all he can to prevent and heal physical and mental disease not only in the name of human science, but also in that of Christ the physician of soul and body. She points out the limits beyond which he must not go if his science and his art are to remain fully human. He may not take life. He may not act against biological law. He can assist nature in the healing process, he may not heal against nature. Hence she forbids surgical interventions against the will of the patient, sterilization of the unfit, any treatment which would heal one abnormality by producing another that is objectionable on moral grounds—certain types of psychological therapy for instance. She is concerned with the totality of human personality in its natural and supernatural aspects.

She has to insist that any technique of artificial insemination that goes counter to this totality is not permissible, however desirable and good may be the end in view. It is objected that this is to look on nature as having certain unalterable structures, whereas scientific method, particularly in medicine, is constantly modifying natural processes for the benefit of the sufferer. Surgery, drugs, therapy of various kinds all redirect or reverse natural processes of degeneration. Why should similar techniques in the sexual sphere be forbidden and the others encouraged? Pius XII in his allocution to the 4th International Congress of

Catholic doctors said: "In the matter of artificial insemination, it is not only advisable to be extremely cautious,
but to refuse it absolutely. This does not necessarily condemn the use of certain artificial means destined solely
either to facilitate the natural act or to assist the natural
act when normally accomplished to attain its end."

The Church obviously holds that the sexual act is a
totality and that to replace it by a surgical technique is
to separate love and the healthy desire for a child from the
physical union which is an integral part of the whole
process of love's expression and so linked to the ultimate
purposes of the married state. On the other hand, she
welcomes any technique which enables intercourse to stand
a chance of being biologically fruitful but she will not
tolerate the suppression of intercourse itself. She insists
that to substitute a surgical technique for the complete
act is to abolish the psychological and personal values and
experiences involved in sexual activity, and to further the
biological process alone. Although the primary end of
sexual union is the birth and education of children, this
end cannot justify a means which so deeply wounds the
personality of the partners.

Yet, when this principle has been established, the problem of the childless couple remains. As the Catholic
doctrine of sexuality and its relation to marriage demands
a strict hierarchy of ends, it would seem that couples who,
through no fault of their own, are infertile are condemned
to a major frustration. Admittedly, as we have already
noted, in such cases the secondary end—the mutual help
husband and wife offer each other—takes the place of the
normal primary end. But is not this a poor substitute for
the rich and vital experience of parenthood? This is no
mere rhetorical or academic question. There are many men
and women in this situation. We believe that a true insight
into the exact nature of their particular vocation reveals a

real call to a type of parenthood that, in its own way and degree, provides ample fulfilment and denies that frustration results inevitably from their biological infertility.

Human beings alone of all the animals can form a genuine society. Marriage possesses in the highest degree the specific characteristic of a society—it is a union of persons for a common activity. Its life is orientated towards two very different ends. The common social purpose is the procreation and education of children. But there is also the end proper to the nature of the human individual—the development of personality which can only be achieved through communion with other persons. The married are called to a mutual sharing of all they can give to each other. This is the meaning of love. Already, then, in this life, they are preparing one another for the Communion of Saints which is offered here and now to all men in substance in the life of the mystical body and will appear in its fullness in the kingdom of the resurrection. The biological end is concerned primarily with this world, while the mutual love of the partners has its roots in eternity and in the world to come. The married union cannot be limited to reproduction, nor can we place the eternal values of married love solely in the spiritual and physical joys of intercourse. These experiences are included in the vast cosmic stream of biological procreation. The love which they express is in another realm altogether, the realm of personal relationships.

The ultimate reality of a shared love remains even if the couple cannot have children. The problem thus becomes that of preventing this love from growing in upon itself. This is a real danger since there are no children to be the visible fruit of sexuality and a guarantee that husband and wife will be offered daily opportunities to increase their love for one another by bringing into its scope those to whom they have given birth and life. Intercourse is the expression of married love but it is not its heart. Adoption, when undertaken for the good of the child, and not solely as a compensation for disappointed hopes, can be of immense value to all the persons concerned.

Adoption is an example of a truly human therapy—as distinct from artificial insemination—based on an act of renunciation and the calm acceptance of an apparently insurmountable physical obstacle to generation. It can do much to develop that full, generous, life-giving love normally made possible and actual by biological parenthood.

Middle age has its own sexual problems. We have space only to make a brief mention of them. There is the danger that once the children have grown up, husband and wife may either revert to a *solitude à deux*, and so cut themselves off from their neighbours to enjoy an unrestrained use of sexuality without fear of pregnancy, or that they may find their love weaken and so seek sexual satisfaction in extra-marital intercourse. The crisis of middle age must be met by a new orientation of love, by a deepening of the whole concept of love and of sexuality as its psychological and physical expression. Unless there is artificial stimulation, the sex urge normally becomes less powerful at this time in the man. Kinsey's data suggest that it remains undiminished in the woman for a much longer period. Nature seems to provide this continued desire so that the woman may now enjoy the pleasure of intercourse without the resulting anxieties and labours of childbirth and motherhood. The husband may have to reckon with this and be willing to cooperate when he has no very strong wish to do so. His own sexuality may need considerable stimulus to be aroused, hence the risk that he may seek this stimulus in younger women, prostitutes or homosexual partners if his love for his wife has lost its warmth and fervour. Outlets such as these are immoral, yet they are evidence of a vital human need which the marriage is no longer fulfilling. Where the couple copulate out of mere habit with no desire or satisfaction, we have a still more tragic situation. The logic of the developing forces of true love should rather make intercourse in middle age still more rich in personal significance and bring with it a pleasure all the more intense because it is the result of a deepening of personal relationships and a decrease of individual egoism.

The inexorable laws of our biological structure bring us at length to old age and the quiescence of sexual passion. The final stage of their life together offers to the married the highest and noblest prize. The shadows and images are about to fade in the light of eternal reality seen face to face. Nothing reveals more clearly the sad deficiencies of our civilization than its attitude of bewildered and blundering helplessness before the problems of old age. The emphasis upon looking back to the past instead of forward to the future, the efforts to make old people feel and act as though they were still young or middle-aged, are pathetic examples of goodwill confused by a failure to see the meaning and vocation of the last stage of life. The gerontologist's casebook with its sad stories of sexual misconduct by the old is evidence of the tragic consequences of this attitude. The problems of old age can only be solved in a religious and family context. Neither religion nor the family are given much encouragement in modern society to bring their immense forces to bear on life in general and old age in particular. The economic and educational structures of western society leave the souls of the old all but naked to the winds of doubt, despair and frustration.

# CHAPTER VIII

# SEX AND GRACE

In our first section we wrote that some thinkers consider man to be an animal who has acquired intelligence and will and so has to control passion by acts of will depending on knowledge. We criticized this view as being an over-simplification. It indeed is, for it takes no account of the revealed fact of the Fall. It does not realize that, however remarkable an instrument the human mind is, its ration-ality is "darkened" by the effects of original sin. It tends, both for good and ill, to be the servant instead of the master of the will. And the will is blown hither and thither by the winds of passion. Even in the highest and apparently least "physical" efforts of the mind—such as its logical proofs of the existence of God—reason works well enough but fails to convince. In his *Contra Gentiles* (I, 4), St Thomas points out that there is always an element of falsity in the workings of reason. For many people things which have been rationally demonstrated remain matters of doubt because it is not everyone who can appreciate the force of a proof. Further, the layman notes that those who are called wise teach different and divergent doctrines. What hope then is there of discovering the truth? More-over there are cases where truths are demonstrated but where there is an element of assertion rather than of proof somewhere in the argument. If this assertion is later shown to be unfounded, then many will reject the whole of the

argument and deny the real facts which it reveals in spite
of the logical inconsistency in one or other of its details.
And hence, says St Thomas, "it was fit that truth concerning divine things should be known with absolute certainty,
by the way of faith".

If this is true of the most fundamental operations of the
mind, how much more is there need, in the realm of behaviour in general and sexual behaviour in particular, of
the light of faith for the intellect and the grace of the
sacraments for the will! How often the efforts of the
Christian to subordinate his sexuality to love are baulked
by failure to appreciate and to use the graces given to him
in baptism, confirmation, matrimony and, above all, in
the Holy Eucharist! Whilst it is only too easy to look on
grace as magic and to expect it to work in us with little
or no cooperation on our part, it is fatal on the other hand
to neglect it and to attempt to organize the passions and
direct them by purely natural means. The apparent success
of unbelievers in ordering their sex lives must not lead us
to suppose they have in fact been without grace. The sacraments are the normal channels of grace, but they do not
bind the generosity of God. As Francis Thompson wrote:

> Some may perhaps with glad surprise,
> Have blundered into Paradise.

We have repeatedly stressed that grace is not only an
individual gift perfecting the personality of the recipient.
This we have done because it is so often forgotten. There
is a true sense in which grace makes us responsible for
others, gives us a share in the redemptive work of Christ.
If the Christian is to live his sex life as God intends he
should, he will need not only the graces granted to him
personally, but the support, understanding and help of all
who like himself are members of Christ, and partakers of
his power and fellow workers with him. If we look on our
spiritual life as a kind of isolated dialogue between our

individual souls and God, we are concentrating on half the truth. As our Lord told St Catherine of Genoa, "Those who love me, love those whom I love."

Catholics are usually given ample instruction on the power of grace in the individual soul. We therefore make no apology for taking such teaching for granted and attempting in these last few pages to see the achievement of a fully human and Christian sexuality as one of the most urgent and important *social* tasks the Christian is called on to do for the glory of God and the good of his fellow men.

In Chapter II we wrote that in Christ we are restored to our first vocation. In him we are again made whole, one with God, one with ourselves, one with others. In him our sexuality returns to the realm of perfect love. This is the truth, however hard it sometimes is to believe. We shall not begin to understand or to achieve a truly human and redeemed sexuality until we see that, whatever the trials, disappointments, failures, our whole effort must be directed to "becoming" what by grace we "are".

Each of the sacraments has its repercussions in the sexual life. When we are baptized, we become members of Christ and of his mystical body. Our own body with all its passions, the bodies of others, which we shall later be tempted to use merely for our own pleasure, are now in their degree united to the body of the God-man and are to be instruments of his redemptive, priestly, prophetic, kingly work. When we are confirmed, the Holy Spirit of love implants in us the force of that divine love which unites the Father and the Son and is destined to coordinate in us the powers of soul and body, reason, will, passion, and to direct them towards the personal and social fulfilment of the unity in mankind which is to mirror the unity in the Godhead of the three Divine Persons. When we receive the sacrament of matrimony, we are given the full

right and duty of using our sexual functions for the love
of God, the expression of our love for husband or wife, the
increase of the race, and of the Church. Above all, we are
made the true image of the union of Christ and the Church.
It is in this infinite, divine context that we have to see our
sexuality. It is in the grace we receive in these three
sacraments that we are to find the strength to achieve the
status which has been given to us in essence, but which
we can only realize in practice by cooperating to the full
with the gift of God.

This is the crux of the whole matter, for in the day-to-
day struggle with self, with the forces of evil within and
around us, it is only too easy to give up, to shut our eyes
to the reality of our redemption, and to sink into despair.
It is essential never to forget that our Lord has accepted
our human condition and saves us from within it. The very
existence of the sacrament of penance, and still more of
the Eucharist, is a constant reminder that he knows our
weakness and our continual need of support and pardon.
However far we may be from a Christian sexuality, however often we fail to show forth in our marriage the union
of Christ and the Church, however often we sin against
love in the use of our sexual powers, all is not lost if we
keep our eyes fixed on the truth and determine to rise
again and to continue the struggle. We sin against God and
men by sexual misconduct, but by rising and returning to
the battle, we honour him and them.

It is above all in the reception of the body and blood
of Christ in Holy Communion that we grasp and receive
the true and eternal reality that lies behind the manifestations of human sexuality. The Eucharist is the sacrament
of union. By it, we are made physically and spiritually one
with him whom we receive and with all his members who
share the communion of his flesh with us. It is a commemoration of his suffering and his redeeming death; it

is the food of those who are on the road from nothingness to eternal glory; it is the pledge and promise of that glory in the life to come. So too, our sexuality, in so far as it is the expression of a pure love of God and of men in their totality, is here and now the servant and food of that love, and in the life to come, when sexual activities in the biological sense will have passed away, the love of which they were the fruitful expression will endure forever.

Chastity, both for the married and for the religious, is a positive and vital force. To look on the Christian sexual code as a mere series of prohibitions, whether the latter are considered essential or preposterous, is to miss the whole point. The negative aspect of the law is a result of the Fall; its essence is contained in the Old Testament text, in which we are told to love God with our whole might and our neighbour as ourself. Christian marriage and the Christian sexual life are perpetual witnesses to the immense dignity of redeemed man and of all his spiritual and physical functions. They derive their inmost meaning from the fact of the Incarnation and are the revealing image of that Incarnation at every time and in every age.

It is obvious that we are living in an era when these realities are unknown or neglected or opposed. In every period of history, man has to reach salvation and wholeness through suffering, pain, struggle and death. It is idle to hanker for some past or future civilization in which the sexual problems are solved by custom. There has never been such a time and there never will be. The Christian's tasks are exacting enough and there is no point in his wasting his energies on a useless nostalgia which only weakens the spirit. His plain duty here and now is to see what sexuality is and means, and then to do all he can to influence every community—family, town, factory, parish, diocese, nation—in favour of a human and Christian attitude to sex. And this must be a positive and corporate undertaking. It is not just a matter of drawing up lists of books, films, plays, advertisements which offend our taste and seem to us to excite to sexual misconduct. These things are symptoms and no disease is attacked at its roots by a therapy which only seeks to suppress its outward manifestations. If the modern world uses sex for lustful purposes, we only make matters far worse by attacking sex itself as though it were a thing to be feared and hated. This is to fall into the same trap as our opponents, for fear and hatred are passions, even though they inhibit rather than prostitute love.

What then is needed is a frontal attack upon the whole anti-Christian position. It is regrettable, we believe, that the first great scientific attempt to discover how people do in fact conduct their sex lives—Kinsey's two projects— should have been the work of non-Catholics. This is not a narrow sectarian remark but rather a confession of failure on the part of Catholics to seize an opportunity for objective study in a field of vital concern to them, since it is so closely involved in the working of a great sacrament. There were doubtless excellent and valid reasons for our absence from this research, yet the fact remains that it is most important that we should know what is the real situation which confronts us in our day and time. The sacraments do not operate in a vacuum. The life of grace is not a Sunday pastime but an affair of every second of every day from the first to the last. It is to be hoped, therefore, that in the English-speaking world as on the European Continent, Catholic moral theologians, psychologists, sexologists, general practitioners, teachers, lawyers, philosophers, confessors and parents should be in the forefront of research, discussion and publication in this battle. The issue is not the defence of middle-class notions of decency or of a morality of convention; it is the formation of a solid doctrine of sexuality based on the facts of revelation and of science.

If we do our duty in this respect, future generations will be aware of a total and fully realistic approach to their sexual problems. Grace will be seen as perfecting not repressing nature. Nature will be seen as crying out for grace. Sexuality will be revealed as the servant of love. The pleasure God has attached to it will appear in its true place, not as something to be ashamed of nor as the chief end to be sought, but as a necessary if subordinate part of a whole process of creative love, whose essence is eternal, however temporary the experiences, sad and joyful, which accompany it in this earthly existence.

Our young people will then know they are surrounded and supported by "a great cloud of witnesses". They will not be alone in a cosmic struggle. They may succumb to the world, the flesh and the devil, but with their eyes open. They will not have the excuse of ignorance or lack of understanding on the part of their elders. They will continue to need our help and encouragement. Men sin through weakness as well as ignorance. They will at least be certain that our help is enlightened and genuine and not the pious claptrap of those who, in the words of La Rochefoucauld, give good advice because they are no longer able to set a bad example.

# SELECT BIBLIOGRAPHY

ATTWATER, Donald (Editor): *Body and Spirit: Essays in Sexuality*, by various writers, London, Longmans, 1939.

FLOOD, Dom Peter (Editor): *New Problems in Medical Ethics*, translated from the French Cahiers Laënnec, volumes 1–3, Cork, Mercier Press, and Westminster, Md, Newman Press, 1953–7.

GIBERT, Henri: *Love in Marriage, The Meaning and Practice of Sexual Love in Christian Marriage*, New York, Hawthorn, 1964.

GUCHTENEERE, R. de: *Judgement on Birth Control*, London and New York, Sheed and Ward, 1943.

GUITTON, Jean: *Essay on Human Love*, London, Rockliff, 1951.

HILDEBRAND, Dietrich von: *In Defence of Purity*, London and New York, Sheed and Ward, 1936.

JOYCE, G. H., S.J.: *Christian Marriage*, London and New York, Sheed and Ward, 1954.

LECLERCQ, Jacques: *Marriage a Great Sacrament*, Dublin, Clonmore and Reynolds and Springfield, Ill., Templegate, 1954.

LEEMING, Bernard, S.J.: *Principles of Sacramental Theology*, London, Longmans, and Westminster, Md, Newman Press, 1956.

McNABB, Vincent, O.P.: *Casti Connubii, Encyclical Letter of Pius XI on Christian Marriage*, with commentary, London and New York, Sheed and Ward, 1933.

MESSENGER, Ernest C.: *Two in One Flesh*, 3 volumes, London, Sands, 1948, and (3 volumes in one) Westminster, Md, Newman Press, 1955.

MURPHY, John P. and John D. Laux: *The Rhythm Way to Family Happiness* (second ed.), New York, Hawthorn, 1959.

ORAISON, Marc.: *Man and Wife: the Physical and Spiritual Foundation of Marriage*, translated by André Humbert, with an Introduction by John Marshall, London, Longmans, 1959, and New York, Macmillan, 1958.

PLÉ, Albert, O.P. (Editor): *Chastity*, translated by Lancelot C. Sheppard (volume 5, "Religious Life Series"), London, Blackfriars, and Westminster, Md, Newman Press, 1955.

SCHEEBEN, Matthias J.: *Mysteries of Christianity*, St Louis, Herder, 1946.

SUTHERLAND, Halliday: *Laws of Life*, London and New York, Sheed and Ward, 1935.

THIBON, Gustave: *What God has Joined Together*, London, Hollis and Carter, and Chicago, Regnery, 1952.

THOMAS, J. L., S.J.: *Marriage and Rhythm*, Westminster, Md, Newman Press, 1957.

WAYNE, T. G.: *Morals and Marriage*, London and New York, Longmans, 2nd edition, 1952.

# The Twentieth Century Encyclopedia of Catholicism

*The number of each volume indicates its place in the over-all series and not the order of publication.*

# TWENTIETH CENTURY ENCYCLOPEDIA OF CATHOLICISM

*Titles are subject to change.*